WHAT A WONDERFUL WORLD

WHAT A WONDERFUL WORLD

Seeing Through New Eyes

By

Ron Chapman

ISBN 1-58961-232-9

Published by PageFree Publishing, Inc.
733 Howard Street
Otsego, MI 49078
www.pagefreepublishing.com

CONTENTS

THE COMMUNITY AROUND US

PERSONALLY AND PRIVATELY

IN RELATIONSHIP

To Sam, Tom, Patrick, and Patricia,
for showing me there are no self-made men.

*An incomplete understanding of any problem or situation
leads to an incomplete solution or action.*

*When understanding is realized,
appropriate solutions and actions become readily apparent.*

WORDS FROM MY DAUGHTER

I have always tried to categorize things, people and events, according to the concepts of "good" and "bad." It always appeared to be easier to systematically arrange things in terms of how I initially saw them. Yet repeatedly these lines were blurred, bent or invisible to me - a definite reminder that we operate in gray scales, and nothing is ever as it seems.

As I worked on Ron's manuscript, my first thoughts were to arrange these anecdotes in times of his life that were "good" and "bad." Alcoholism is obviously "bad," and divorce, that's "bad" too. Yet I couldn't help but notice that these supposedly negative events and times yielded wonderful lessons, new situations, and for Ron and me, a much better relationship. For years we struggled with how to relate as parent and child and with the ability to co-exist in the same household peacefully, because Ron filled the difficult position of live-in stepparent.

Ron and my mother divorced during my sophomore year of college, and at the time it seemed like the worst possible thing that could ever happen. The divorce was a worst fear being realized; I was being propelled into uncertainty and instability. No one saw it coming, and no third-person observer viewed it as a relief or as something that needed to happen, as is so often the case with divorce.

Yet I look back at that time and I do not categorize it as "bad." In the few years since the divorce a wonderful change has occurred. I can sense a new peace and happiness in each of my parents, and this has transcended their relationships with my sister and me. Ron and I have moved past our tumultuous beginning, forming a good relationship where the things that we used to fight about no longer exist as issues.

Working on this manuscript solidified that realization for me. So often I was reading the pieces thinking, "Where was I during all of this?" and wishing that I had paid more attention. But as hindsight is always 20/20, looking back even now, I realize that this event of Ron's presence in our lives cannot be categorized according to my "good" and "bad" scale. It is neither, it is both, it is, and has been, a tremendous blessing and learning experience.

I hope that as you read through these stories, observations, insights and lessons that you will share the same experiences that we have in coming to terms with the multi-faceted and complicated nature of the world we live in. Nothing is as it seems, and all things happen for a reason. This is the only certainty, and it is neither "good" nor "bad."

-Natalie Marie Solomon

INTRODUCTION

DURING a walk early this morning, I noticed that a large flock of pigeons that roosts atop a local business near my home was no longer to be found. I searched for clues, finding none.

My mind scrolled through the possibilities with a crescendo of commentary. *Pigeons don't just up and move. They must have been exterminated as pests. Some call them winged rats. Properly, they are known as rock doves and are quite lovely. Surely they didn't kill them. But there were a bunch of them. Maybe they relocated them. Maybe they scared them away. Unlikely. The last time I tried to scare a flock of pigeons it was hopeless. That was delightful, the girls, Regina and I running around on top of the shopping center with water guns. I hate it when animals get killed irreverently. All they're doing is making a home out of convenient circumstances. But they are a mess.*

The amazing part of the story has nothing to do with pigeons, though I do find them beautiful. Rather it is about my awareness, of a change in the world around me, of the many possibilities, of my own thoughts…all mirrored as change within.

Just before the pigeon incident, I had been practicing "not knowing." This means I was walking and practicing seeing without my normal opinions and conclusions. For example, I might look at a tree and try to relinquish what I know of it, seeing only a thing rather than categorizing it as a cottonwood, green, tall, or even as a tree.

Sometimes it's surprising what I see when I relinquish that which I believe I know. It can be as simple as releasing the information about something, or as difficult as examining my beliefs and opinions. But my experience is that, beyond the things I think I know, lies uncharted territory because what I know, or think I know, obstructs my ability to see clearly.

I've come to understand that the Divine, in the form of insight, intuition and creation, is beyond our ability to manage or control, entering our Being through the Mind, then interpreted through mental faculties. Certainly, the amazing things I've seen in my own life as well as the lives of others suggest there is something to be tapped. And it seems to be available only after our knowledge and certainties are set aside.

My experience has also shown me that this is the realm of unlimited possibilities, the fertile and perhaps holy ground of awe, reverence, beauty, truth and miracles. In my work as a consultant and mentor, I have been routinely dumbfounded by the transformations such seeing can produce. More significantly, I've been humbled by the extraordinary changes in my own life from the same such sight.

The material in *What a Wonderful World* offers an opportunity to question, and the possibility to not only see through new eyes but perhaps to experience anew. It is no more than a beginning, and is not for those seeking the proverbial "easier, softer way." Personal awakening is daunting and demanding work. Yet from my experience and point of view, there is no other work to be done because there is no "easier, softer way." It is only an illusion, a kind of spiritual and psychological fool's gold.

Speaking of delusions, it is important for me to note a few of my own, and to do so in the context of acknowledgment. Thank you to Mari Selby for aiding me in finally coming to see "me." Without her counsel this book could not have come into being, because I was blind about myself and the realm of marketing. She guided me unerringly through an organic process that was highly effective.

Thank you too, to my daughter, Natalie. She reviewed and compiled endless material, bringing order from chaos, which was, also, beyond me. I'm simply not a very good judge of my own work.

Just a word about the questioning exercises which are offered throughout the book. If you are like me, you might not see the benefit of such effort. Usually I think by simply reading something, I understand it. That's yet another delusion; only a small percentage of that which we read actually takes hold within us. The full effect of reading comes from working with the ideas and information. Thus the inclusion of questions and opportunities for you to write are intended to aid in internalizing ideas. You may want to consider trying them to see if they are beneficial. Just remember, often benefits are not readily seen except in retrospect.

So read on. See what you see. Feel what you feel. Come to know what you know, and what you don't.

There are surprises waiting. That's the most exciting (and fun) part. Be curious. Explore your own inner terrain using the outer as mirror. See differently and more clearly. Examine yourself, perhaps much to your surprise. Consider the role of God in places and ways often not seen.

And best of all, see as little children do, with wonder, and with gratitude. There is something extraordinary around us all the time. It is called life, and it is typically not what we think.

-Ron Chapman

Afterthoughts

Two weeks have passed since writing the words above. This morning, the pigeons were ensconced once more in their rooftop roost.

I laughed when I saw them. All my thoughts were off the mark. For some inexplicable reason, the flock had disappeared and returned - proof that even my best thinking is suspect at times. Also it was a powerful reminder that seeing anew is something that occurs beyond my control.

"The important thing is to not stop questioning." - Albert Einstein

WHAT A WONDERFUL WORLD

"I see trees of green, red roses too. I'll watch them bloom, for me and you. And I think to myself…what a wonderful world." - Louis Armstrong

****

I may not be Louis Armstrong, but there is so much to be grateful for in this wonderful world. Armstrong knew that and sang about everything from blue skies to babies crying, always returning to the refrain: "What a wonderful world!"

In the pages of this essay, I offer a few ideas to consider…ideas about this wonderful world, and especially, the gratitude with which Armstrong sang so eloquently.

I will begin with Brother Pete. He is a Dominican Brother and a good friend. I have learned an immense amount from Brother Pete through his unending mantra of "Turning your attitude to gratitude." Especially, I learned that we cannot just make ourselves feel grateful on demand. Imagine enduring the death of a loved one, a serious illness, or loss of a job, and saying, "I think I'll be grateful." Such an approach simply doesn't work for most of us. More often than not the path to gratitude lies in seeing with new eyes.

I once discussed this very subject with my life mentor, Sam, as we walked around his hometown in Texas. He asked me for an example, and at that moment a frog hopped into the roadway. A car raced by us and the result was a Frisbee frog.

I used that as my example. "Sam, how can I be grateful for the death of that frog?"

He grinned at me. "Why Ron, if frogs didn't die we'd be up to our asses in them."

Imagine a world filled with frogs! Maybe death is something for which we can be grateful. Perhaps there are many things to see with gratitude that don't normally appear as such.

Eighteen years ago, my first wife, Melanie, left me. Shortly thereafter, I was forced from a career. I certainly was not grateful, but I was compelled to confront my alcoholism.

I understand today that I could not be living the extraordinary life I am living had I not dealt with the problem. And, I would not have done so were it not for the duress of abandonment and lost career.

Because I see these matters in a new light, the light of understanding, I am exceedingly grateful today. This is even true for the alcoholism, which precipitated the situation.

Taking matters still further, what of the common occurrences of our daily lives, which often escape our notice? For example, what is the value of our senses? How much compensation would any of us ask if we were to forfeit eyesight or hearing in this instant? What is it worth to be able to see and hear?

Dr. Norman Dawson, a good friend, lost his hearing three decades ago, regaining it two years ago through surgery. He says that the chance to hear music or a human voice is priceless.

And what of the abundance in our lives? We have so very, very much. Or, for that matter, the people in our lives? Think of the countless, beautiful faces of friends, family and loved ones.

What have we done to warrant such gifts as these in our lives? And, make no mistake; they are gifts, like the proverbial manna from heaven.

I have another friend who is well worth mentioning. Patrick was retrieved from the bowels of society, a hopeless alcoholic. Today he is twenty-three years clean and sober, making significant contributions to life.

Patrick says, "Gratitude is an action, not a feeling." He would challenge us, "What good is gratitude if we cannot and do not express it unless it happens to feel good?"

We've all heard the story of Nelson Mandela, who was falsely imprisoned for twenty-seven years. On the day of his release he thanked his captors because the experience had taught him that no one could take away his happiness or well being. Imagine, twenty-seven years wronged and being able to act gratefully to those who wronged you.

There is another powerful idea related to this subject. The fastest way to lose any gift is to fail to see that it is a gift; taking it for granted and doing nothing to maintain it. Therein lies the secret as to why we might want to act grateful even when we do not feel grateful.

Life and everything in it is a privilege - not a right, and certainly not something we have earned. It is a gift, a priceless and precious gift.

Take a moment and look around you. Notice the abundance that is clearly represented. Notice or imagine the beautiful faces of friends and loved ones. Imagine the freedom that permits so much of this, and the senses that allow us to experience it. Imagine life itself as a great gift.

Do you feel grateful?

Do you see that it matters not whether we feel grateful for anything? It is only important that we see with a new light in our eyes…to find ways to act out our gratitude. To desire that gratitude above all else, and thus to understand it is all part of a wonderful world.

Afterthoughts

In the culmination of many years of work, I had need to write a speech that effectively expressed the awe I felt. This was that speech. It captures the sense of gratitude that inevitably follows the experience of seeing anew. In the final analysis, I find I have only two authentic responses to seeing the truth. The first is gratitude. The second is humor. If I am experiencing neither of these, I have not yet seen the truth.

THE COMMUNITY AROUND US

CELEBRATE DIVERSITY

ONE afternoon, as I drove around the city of Albuquerque on errands, I stopped for a cold drink at a convenience store. While exiting with soda in hand, a stocky fellow holding a bag of crushed ice opened the door for me. We began to chat as we crossed the parking lot.

As we approached a dark blue tractor-trailer rig I heard a great commotion, the deranged barking of dogs. I glanced up. Framed in the window of the truck were two ugly little faces, black halves split by a spit of white and balanced with two pointed ears. Boston terriers.

I felt a smile creep to my face and out of the side of my eye noticed my companion waving to the dogs. The racket increased as I turned and saw a grin on his face.

"Is that your truck?" I asked.

The man's grin widened further as he nodded with obvious pleasure.

Curious, I inquired further. "What in the world are you doing with two Boston Terriers in your truck?"

The trucker stopped and turned to me. "That rig's home," he said. "They never knowed anyplace else."

"No shit!" I replied.

Encouraged by my enthusiastic response, the man chuckled before continuing, "Yep. The female on the left. She's got more 'n a million miles on her."

I laughed with delight, spurring him on further.

"And the puppy there, he's only been with me 'bout a year." A twinkle came into his eyes followed by a huge grin. "He's gettin' near a hunnerd thousand."

The trucker joined me in laughing as we shook hands. He went forward to open the door and the terriers escalated their antics, barking and dancing. The man turned with a sheepish look and announced, "They's pretty happy. But they's also protectin' their home."

I nodded once more, then waved a friendly farewell.

As I drove away I glanced up to see one ugly little dog watching me.

A moment later as I idled at a stoplight, I noticed a bumper sticker. It was bright yellow with a brilliant rainbow perfectly centered. In puffy white letters was the phrase, "Celebrate Diversity."

For some inexplicable reason, a thought raced through my mind. I realized that I had just experienced diversity. That diversity was more than race, creed or nationality. We are surrounded by extraordinary diversity every day of our lives. It is a kind of diversity that contributes to our lives.

Then, unbidden, a rush of memories poured through my mind. People. The amazing people who had shaped me and participated in my life.

I remembered my friend Patrick as we stood in church during the closing prayer when the congregation clasped hands to say The Lord's Prayer. His deep voice resonated, "Our Father, who art in heaven…" An elbow jabbed into my side as Patrick sought my attention. "…Howard be Thy name…"

Patrick laughed freely and loudly at his joke as others turned to watch. My face flushed crimson though I could not stifle giggles in response to his humorous and sacrilegious contribution.

Who knows what possessed him to let me in on his secret that day, but it was exhilarating.

Dr. Anna Lupps then came to mind as she listened to my complaints of discouragement with my life. She had reversed the ill effects of conventional medicine on a liver dysfunction with her exceptional grasp of holistic medicine and had become a comforting confidante.

Her gutteral, northern European dialect clipped her words as she told me, "Ron, you're thirty-three years old. Even Gandhi had to wait until his mid-fifties before he made a contribution. Maybe you should just chill out a bit."

I recall the irony that an Oklahoma boy should find himself in a holistic physician's office being told to chill out.

A glimpse of a portrait of Clovis Burden followed, hunkered down on his heels, tobacco juice cup in hand as he studied the practice of my junior high school football team. His disciplined approach to coaching taught me a great deal about perseverance and the value of hard work.

Recollections scrolled through my mind as I waited for the traffic light to change. Like an unending movie reel, countless people passed through my mind's eye. Each represented a single element of this thing called diversity.

The last memory was of a recent conversation with an elderly friend. Jim calls himself "the luckiest s.o.b. alive." Indeed, his life seems to bear that out.

Jim is a survivor of D-Day, the beaches of Normandy. More amazing still is that he served on the frontline of the entire push from Omaha Beach to the heart of Germany and the Nazi surrender. Physically unscathed, Jim returned to the United States and a courtship with alcoholism that drove him to the brink of death. He relates how he awoke in a solitary confinement pit at the Kansas State Penitentiary: naked, hungry and without fingernails which had fallen out as a result of alcoholism and insanity.

Jim says he had a spiritual experience in prison, an experience that struck him both sober and sane. That condition has been maintained for more than fifty years. He claims no credit for this seeming miracle.

When Jim is among friends, he invariably will say, "I'm so grateful to be here with all my clothes on and in my right mind." We always respond, "So are we, Jim."

The traffic light changed and I drove forward, following the car with the bumper sticker. My reverie surprised me, as did the realization that resulted.

I saw that diversity is not what it's come to mean. Diversity is of God. Spirit adores diversity. No two snowflakes are alike. In a few square feet of prairie may be dozens of strains of grasses. Rain forests testify to the breadth of forms nature nurtures.

Each of us is blessed to be surrounded by every imaginable type of person bearing the full range of human experience. We are the products and beneficiaries of an extraordinary opportunity.

Celebrate diversity? Celebrate indeed!

Afterthoughts

The story demonstrates that moments of insight are akin to lightning: beyond my control and striking in a moment's notice. They follow rules beyond my ability to comprehend, or perhaps even to see.

Questions to Consider

When has a brilliant insight or epiphany come to me? What was revealed? Have I been compelled to act as a result of it, or simply satisfied in the knowing? If action ensued, was I the actor or was I acted upon?

_____

_____

_____

_____

_____

_____

_____

_____

ONE STORY IN A COMMUNITY

IN retrospect, it was an odd setting to observe community. I sat in a sterile, cell-like room with white plaster walls and a twelve-foot ceiling from which an ancient paddle fan hung, slowly turning.

I was in a small town in the valley of the Rio Grande at the request of a friend, Michael, to attend a small support group. We gorged ourselves on chile rellenos and enchiladas at a local cafe, then walked to the large, rambling community center. It was a warm gusty night. The building creaked as we entered, and the wind moaned as it bore the rich scent of the earth through massive cottonwoods surrounding the building.

I sat in a metal folding chair beside Michael amid six local people, four men and two women seated around a table. There was a worn and weary look to them. I spied mud caked boots, nicotine stained fingers, and massive silver bracelets and belt buckles inlaid with turquoise.

A moment before the hour and the beginning of the meeting, the heavy silence was ruptured by a door banging shut followed by the sound of heavy, irregular foot falls echoing through the entry hall. My eyes moved quickly to the door as a large, barrel-chested man appeared. He was a rough looking fellow, calloused and creased, skin burned dark red by the sun.

Clutched to his chest, in strange contrast to his rugged appearance, was a gray miniature poodle clad in a Kelly green sweater. The dog had a bad haircut with a ridge upon its head like an overgrown Mohawk.

The man limped into the room, shifted the dog to one arm, and then grabbed a plastic jug filled with cookies from the table top. He moved slowly to the end of the table and placed the cookies before a seat. Crossing the room, he drew a cup of water at the washbasin in the corner. Returning, he eased himself onto the chair and carefully set the poodle upon the table.

The meeting began while I watched in disbelief as the man fed cookies to the dog. The animal's delighted chomping and smacking seemed to hang before the group and caused Michael to burst into laughter. I grinned but noticed the others studying the floor in seeming embarrassment.

The meeting unfolded slowly. The dog wolfed cookies and occasionally lowered its head to the cup, loudly lapping water. Tail wagging; he ate his fill as he glanced around the room. After a time, with a full belly, he lay down upon the table and rested his head on his paws.

The man said nothing and no one looked toward him. Not one word was uttered about the poodle. The dynamics of the group intrigued me.

The man finally spoke with only a few minutes remaining. He did not address the subject of the meeting. Instead, he told a brief version of his life story, a tale of hardship, woe and misfortune. Serving in a war had damaged him. He slept poorly and had driven two wives and several children from him. He admitted to being embittered and angry. His life had not turned out as planned.

I glanced around the room. All eyes were riveted on him, the people listening with rapt attention. His story intimated that he was a regular at this group. He was no stranger. I understood he had told his life story over and over again. Still they heard him, listening carefully.

The man finished by explaining that he was incapable of maintaining a relationship with anyone except his dog. The poodle was the joy of his life and, at times, the only source of comfort to him. As his words faded, I watched his coarse hands gently caress the ears of his beloved companion.

The meeting adjourned and the dog leapt to the floor, greeting everyone present with a sniff and a wag of his tail. The man followed his poodle but spoke to no one. At the door, the man leaned down painfully and lifted the dog into his arms. As he walked out, I watched his brawny limping figure.

The last I saw was the head of the poodle with a lousy haircut, cradled in the man's arms. Black eyes studied me carefully. He blinked and was gone.

Beneath everything lies a story. I had observed a part of the fabric of a community. It was not what I expected.

Afterthoughts

It is said that if we understood all, we would forgive all. This experience with the man and his dog helped me to realize there are no exceptions to this notion, because there is nothing to forgive. Each time I see this, I find myself humbled...and immersed in community which is nothing more than the state between people which occurs when impediments are removed.

Questions to Consider

Do I seek to understand? Does forgiveness come as a result? Where does my vision seem to be obstructed, where am I judgmental or critical? Do I want to see anew? How does this affect me and my role in community?

_____

_____

_____

_____

_____

_____

_____

SPEED BUMPS

ON a long walk this weekend with my faithful companion Lucy, our nearly blind Chinese pug, I was delighted to discover that the city had added a series of speed bumps to the roadbed. Actually these were more of the speed "hump" variety in that they do not bring cars to a standstill, seeking rather to force slower speeds upon traffic. I am not surprised by the project since people routinely race through the neighborhood at fifty miles per hour, or more, despite a posted speed limit of thirty.

My delight at the addition stems primarily from the fear I routinely experience in response to speeding vehicles on residential streets. I must admit that a number of encounters have surprised me: the teenager who flipped me off when I motioned for her to slow down as I ran to grab my elderly pug, Buster, from the road; the small business owner who typically zips through our child-rich neighborhood at high speeds; the adolescent boy who races his four wheeler around the block but only once at a time because he knows a parent will chase him down and chastise him; and the increasing number of adult women who have adopted the highly aggressive driving tendencies formerly reserved to men.

As I walked, admiring the new speed humps and relishing the obvious consternation of many drivers encountering them, a thought came to me. "Those who abuse a privilege of society will have that same privilege forfeited by society."

An underlying principle of society is that certain rights and privileges are conferred upon members of the society. In fact, I am of the opinion that despite our supposed constitutional rights, everything we are granted by society is a privilege. We may argue that each of us has some basic rights but every society establishes processes whereby any of those may be forfeited for sufficient cause including our life through death penalties, our livelihood through expulsion from a trade or profession, our belonging through retraction of membership, or our pursuit of happiness and well being through incarceration.

Speed bumps are a simple but obvious reminder of the ease with which our freedom can be limited and retracted by the society to which we belong. They also demonstrate the importance of valuing such privileges at the same time that we accept the responsibility that is equally and simultaneously conferred with the granting of the privilege. In the end, when we see our good fortune in receiving such benefits, we may be able to accept them gratefully and graciously, honoring the intent through our own behavior.

I'm sure these thoughts are not on the minds of the drivers now inconvenienced by the speed bumps in the neighborhood. Perhaps they should be. Our thoughtlessness often precipitates losses we would just as soon avoid.

Afterthoughts

My usual reaction to impediments is to battle them. It's hard for me to see that resistance is a naturally occurring force, and often quite valuable.

Questions to Consider

Thinking back to a recent impediment in my life, whether as a relationship obstacle, a personal challenge, or the simple thwarting of my wishes or desires…did I resist? Why or why not? Did I perceive that resistance would be successful? Did I learn anything from the experience? Does willpower work in resistance? What is the proper use of such will, if any?

HOGARES DEL VALLE

I recently had the privilege of speaking at Hogares del Valle, a youth residential treatment facility on the mesa southwest of Albuquerque. The young men and women range in age from thirteen to seventeen and have been mandated to spend time there as a result of substance abuse problems. For many of them, Hogares is a last chance to redirect their lives. More than a few have opted for this program rather than being sent to youth detention facilities or other forms of incarceration.

The most striking impression was the enthusiasm and engaging attitude the teens displayed. They're taught to be open, to be courteous, and to seek assistance. These kids are not at all what one expects from troubled youth. But then the only expectation we would have is that formed in our minds by the media, and that is notoriously negative toward both youth and substance abuse.

Their naiveté as well as their genuinely good intentions stunned me. These were not the gangsters and troublemakers we've been lead to expect. In all honesty, despite a fairly wide level of involvement with youth for more than six years, I'm still waiting to encounter the kind of kids our society has been taught to fear.

I remembered the provocative film, *Traffic*. If you would like to see the real kids at the heart of the drug problem, rent the movie. Of course, you'll probably be quite troubled by what you see. The young woman swept into the drug vortex at the heart of the plot is a distressingly normal teenager. So were those at Hogares del Valle.

One of the truths about prejudice and misunderstanding is that when we encounter the supposed enemy and find them to be remarkably similar to us, it alters our perception of the problem. This has been true in wars when soldiers from opposing armies come to see each other as no longer evil, or when racial lies are revealed as a result of an encounter with someone with a different skin color, or when a conversation with someone of a different creed demonstrates their similarity to us rather than their differences.

All these thoughts and more raced through me as I began to speak. I told them the truth. I told them I was an adult who could not forget the pain and torment of my own youth, explaining that the world viewed me as a successful adult male. Then the facts of my life rushed out: several feigned suicide attempts, alcoholism, divorce, loss of a career, and a profound fear that I was an abject failure. I recounted how all my life I had felt apart from others, convinced that I was beyond repair or redemption.

Tears filled my eyes as I described the hope I now feel. I have been made whole, and it is an extraordinary and precious gift.

Then we talked. I felt the presence of the Divine descend into the midst of our communion of brokenness. A profound feeling of love swept through me.

As I departed, I suggested they each spend a moment gazing into my eyes. I wanted them to see the love that poured through me, softened by troubles and failure. And I wanted them to know they were perfect.

Reflecting as I drove homeward, I knew these young people faced a terrible challenge. The relapse rate for substance abusers is tragically high. And despite a great deal of education in recent decades, we still consider people with alcohol or drug problems to be choosing their fate…morally deficient.

I must honestly tell you that an encounter with kids such as these will challenge those notions. At a minimum it will reveal our ignorance. At most it will demonstrate our hypocrisy and prejudices.

My heart ached for those young people; I anguished over their dilemma. There are no simple solutions. Time. Energy. Resources. Compassion. Dedication. Even these may not succeed. In the end, our only strategy may be to love them and offer our hands and our hope.

Afterthoughts

I once asked a wise woman, Betsy Comstock, how I could avoid failing at life. After a long pause, she said, "Continue to be willing to grow. And remember, knowledge comes from the most unlikely sources."

Only a few days later, I responded to a knock at my front door and found two Jehovah's Witnesses. I felt hackles rise, but somehow recalled Betsy's words. With great reluctance, I invited them in for tea. We spent an hour in a lovely conversation. I remember that I learned a few things that day, though I cannot now recall the nature of the learning, only that I had to swallow my intolerance and arrogance in order to do so.

Questions to Consider

It is said, "There but for the grace of God, go I." Can I see myself in undesirable circumstances? Why or why not, and to whose credit? While I may have toiled in my own right, can I also see my good fortune?

_____

_____

_____

_____

_____

_____

_____

LATE NIGHT EMERGENCY

I once spent several hours in a late night emergency room, from late night into the early morning hours. It was just another home improvement casualty, a laceration across the top of my foot. My wife, Regina, and I came prepared with a newspaper, novels, and some planning work. After all, emergency room visits can become marathons.

It is strange how the emergency room is quite unlike cinema and television portrayals, an endless stream of the tedious rather than constant drama suffused with romance. Still there is an odd contrast, calm, businesslike workers opposite a crisis, or at least each patient's perceived crisis. I suspect this must be a source of exasperation for those patients and their loved ones, imagining this lack of dramatic response to their problems to be a sign of disinterest or distraction. Yet, even the expressed frustrations are taken in stride.

My wife and I chatted while we waited and watched the stream of brokenness and fragility. A wearied emaciated woman sat with her head propped in her hand, her mother bedraggled beside her. Two young couples bickered and fought. A few, tear-stained faces shone amid the numbing lethargy of endless late night television chatter. The unceasing flow of humanity never ends.

Surprisingly, after a reasonable wait I was brought to a treatment room, accepted ahead of several others. My escort explained that my injury was real and warranted attention ahead of the drunks fearful of excessive vomiting and others with coughs, bumps, and phantom aches. Even now, that sounds callous. But I suspect from the faces I saw, that many emergency room visitors live in some degree of fear and loneliness. Unfortunately, emergency rooms are ill equipped to respond to inner human needs. Treat the presenting ailments and move on. Time and experience must surely desensitize the staff.

My nurse, a pleasant man in his early forties, was a veteran of many urban emergency and critical care wards. Our conversation ebbed and flowed around ambulance arrivals and searches for surgical supplies. He was quite genuine, though I admit to being intrigued by his almost casual acceptance and humor about trauma and death. As we spoke, a chink appeared in the armor of his professional demeanor. He cared deeply about the dilemmas of advanced medical care and the spiritually demeaning quality of some practices. How can you revive an elderly man in good conscience even in response to his family's wishes when he is doomed by pulmonary obstruction and tumors? In the face of such decisions, which may undermine the very dignity they are committed to save, they muddle along with efficient medical practices.

I think it a tribute that questions are not swept under an emotional rug, even as the work goes on. Our lives are not intended to be simple. We must ever grapple with hopeless questions and confusing dilemmas. After being challenged, we can arise in newfound wisdom and strength. There is virtue in the struggle.

The suturing done and the paperwork complete, my nurse's shift had ended as he finished repairing my torn foot. On his way out he showed me his reading material, a book of travel, perhaps to transport him away, and a bilingual magazine to help him learn Spanish. We shook hands as I informed him that I might chronicle the night. He laughed and gestured in a way that clearly expressed his doubts. I think he thought it all to be terribly mundane and commonplace. Perhaps, but I have heard it said that the extraordinary is often obscured amid seemingly uninteresting details, waiting to be revealed.

Afterthoughts

I have been told it is a sign of advancement to experience "vital interest" in the matters of the day. Such vital interest comes when the veil of my self-interest is pierced. It is curious and dispassionate, observing rather than participating.

Questions to Consider

Who and what is around me? What's really going on? What is my purpose in relation to it? What are my available choices? Is there a contribution to be made? To whom and to what end? What then is the measure of me?

_____
_____
_____
_____
_____
_____
_____
_____

A PUMPKIN TALE

IT was October, the harvest month, and I sat upon a bale of straw watching the activities of a farm store in the valley of the Rio Grande north of Albuquerque. The late afternoon sun was warm. Despite the long shadows of the cottonwoods, the air was heavy with the scent of sunshine upon the straw and the verdant odors of new mown hay and manure. Stray aromas wafted by me, roasting green chile and cinnamon in hot, mulled cider. Beneath a fragile blue sky, New Mexico sunflowers shimmered, their lines sharp and distinct in the dry air. There was a dull drone of busyness and children playing. Somewhere in the distance a donkey brayed. The setting was rich and overwhelming to the senses.

Across the yard an old woman watched me watching her. She rocked gently in a chair in the shade of the verandah. A brilliant Navajo blanket draped her shoulders and her graying hair was pulled neatly into a bun atop her head. With great care and patience she raised a large mug to her lips and sipped gingerly. Her eyes studied me as she slowly lowered the mug in lightly quaking hands.

My attention swung to a man and woman selecting pumpkins from a flatbed trailer with their little boy. The mellow orange globes stirred thoughts of jack-o-lanterns and pumpkin pie, food for soul and body. The boy waved a caramel-coated apple toward a monstrous squash; it must have weighed seventy-five pounds. His parents sought to dissuade him from his choice. I imagined the parents' consternation, for a three-foot tall jack-o-lantern would be quite daunting.

The boy became agitated and began to stomp his feet while waving the apple with great energy. He jerked his arm and I watched in amazement as the apple launched from the impaling popsicle stick and struck a tall gaunt farmer upon the arm. He turned quickly and surveyed the scene as he walked toward the boy. Flushed with embarrassment, the man and his wife gestured apologetically. The farmer was silent as he folded lanky knees and squatted beside the boy. Wiping caramel from his forearm with a handkerchief, he spoke with the now subdued boy.

The parents watched quizzically. After a few moments, the farmer rose as he balanced himself with one hand placed lightly upon the boy's shoulder. He motioned across the yard with his free hand, beckoning two sturdy young men who came at a trot. The parents fidgeted as I began to understand. The men lifted the giant pumpkin onto a cart and headed toward the parking lot followed by the little boy skipping gaily and grinning from ear to ear.

The boy's father extracted his billfold but the farmer shook his head while motioning for him to cease. He patiently nodded and smiled until the man and woman retreated, doggedly following the huge orange orb toward their car. It seems the pumpkin was their penance for an unruly son. Or, he may not have intended punishment, only the granting of a little boy's wish.

The raucous cries of crows caused me to look back across the yard. The old woman smiled at me from her rocker. She had been watching the scene and nodded her head in acknowledgment. The day seemed dreamlike then. I rose and followed my nose and stomach to hot, buttered sweet corn. Heavily salted, it was the perfect complement to the day. Then, I drank deeply from a cup of cider, which bathed my mouth in sweetness.

The boy will remember that day for a lifetime, while the pumpkin shall vanish into the earth from whence it came. In the tales he will tell it will grow larger and larger until its proportions shall match the magnificence of the event, though its size will be inflated. You may be assured; October will be his favorite month.

Afterthoughts

I am struck by the clarity of the memory of this event with the pumpkin. It was one of those moments when I was raptly attentive to the world around me, much to my delight.

During my morning walk today, I noticed that I've not been paying attention lately. I had fallen into the busyness of the mind and the certainty of knowing my surroundings. As soon as I noticed it, I found myself captivated by bees droning around a spear of yucca blossoms. I was awake once more.

Questions to Consider

What event or circumstance recently brought me into the moment? Were there other affairs distracting me from the present? Why?

_____

_____

_____

_____

_____

_____

_____

HOMELESSNESS

MANY years ago, homeless beggars who assailed me on the streets offended me. I thought them tactless and a blight on society.

Then fifteen years ago I found myself seated in a classroom pursuing a graduate degree in social welfare after a decade spent in the corporate business community. I intended to take my business skills into social services and try to improve the appalling condition of service delivery.

A professor challenged us to examine our biases, and by the end of the term, after much inner reflection, I realized I was fearful where the homeless were concerned. They represented the failure I had managed to avoid through hard work, but mostly by good luck in the genetic game of roulette and the good fortune to be born into a home that allowed me to learn and excel. I came to see that their street corner presence was a mirror into my own fears, and that my discomfort came from within.

I remember especially one lecture, when the same professor told us that the homeless deserved the dignity of a few bucks in their pocket to be spent however they wished, even for a drink or a smoke. She said that we have no right to judge them so harshly as to withhold the freedom of choice granted all members of a democratic society.

It was shortly thereafter that I began to engage the street people, to look them in the eye, giving freely if I felt like it, declining if I wished, and chatting with them about where they are from, where they are bound, and what happened to them. My discomfort melted.

Sometime later I participated in a Sunday church service at a shelter. I watched as we forced hungry people to endure a service, and then doled out food. I knew it was wrong to visit our religious convictions upon others before tending to their hunger. Jesus would have been appalled.

Shortly thereafter, I happened to become a part of the creation of an organization called ArtStreet. The feature to which I was most enamored was the goal of eliminating the barriers between homeless people and the community at large. It is really quite simple. When community members engage the homeless and near homeless, they find ordinary people, struggling to be sure, but for the most part men, women, and children who fall well within the bounds of normal. This dose of reality seems to dissolve the ignorance and fear that lies beneath indignation, righteousness, and discomfort.

Better still, the homeless individuals must begin to relinquish their self-perception of apartness. It is difficult to maintain an illusion of defectiveness and deficiency when others cease to see you as inadequate. The experience reminds me of an old Andy Griffith show when Otis, the town drunk and local image of lack, would show up on Friday night and lock himself in the jail cell. Andy and Barney, the local law enforcement duo, would welcome him and then get on with their business. The portrait was one of normalcy and acceptance.

Homelessness. It is nothing more than one part of a community that should neither be indulged nor denied. neither encouraged nor discouraged. We are all in this together. Most of us are quite lucky. We've been blessed with good fortune, often through no great credit to us.

Afterthoughts

I continue to see a vacillation within me between engagement and retreat with regard to the homeless. Sometimes I simply cannot muster compassion. The best I can do is to forgive myself.

Questions to Consider

Thinking back to a recent offense or resentment, what would it mean to forgive it? Why do I feel this way? And what must I forgive within me in order for the slate to be clean? What would it be like for me to be without fault? How would I feel?

_____

_____

_____

_____

_____

_____

_____

_____

EVENING GRACE

MY wife, Regina, and I sat on our back porch into the evening as summer waned, watching the onset of darkness. At some point our conversation diverged onto a topic to which we often seem drawn: moving to a small town.

The thought of moving caused me to survey the yard around us. It was an amazing product of years spent brainstorming that included fruit trees, a berry patch, brick walkways, a sitting garden, bird feeders and a small pool for toads. I recalled words my father once uttered with pride but tinged with the sadness of reality, "I've planted trees from coast to coast and never once stayed long enough to see them fully matured."

So it is with our increasingly transient, upwardly mobile society. The pace of our movement is so rapid that the passage of time in our own yards is a mystery to many of us. I have been like my father, residing in nineteen places in forty years, an average of slightly more than two years per place. Granted, some changes were between adjacent neighborhoods or across towns, still they were moves with all their associated uprooting.

From some grand perspective I must appear manic as I dash about frantically, at each arrival undertaking to construct a long-term residence in a flurry of projects and improvements, only to relocate once more. In my mind each change is for good reason or just cause.

I remember a visit to Regina's uncle's home near old town Albuquerque. Born and raised within blocks of his house, her Uncle Mickey is a fixture of the area. His backyard confirms years spent in a single place with a coop housing their chicken Carlotta, fully mature plum and peach trees, garden convoluted by inspirations over years, well established shade trees, stepping stones, an extension to the verandah and a concrete walkway in the process of being dug and poured. There is an ease of living in his home that has been cultivated over decades of daily rituals.

Regina often relates the story of visits to her maternal grandparents' home in the rural, agricultural valley of Chimayo in Northern New Mexico. Evenings were spent beneath towering cottonwoods between the tin-roofed, adobe house and the acequia, the irrigation ditch that brought water to crops, orchards and livestock.

She and her sisters played in the flowing water amid the sound of crickets and frogs as the adults sat smoking and chatting over strong, black coffee. The routine varied little over time though bodies aged and children grew. Regina vividly recalls the glow of their hand rolled cigarettes in the dark and the odor of burning tobacco. All too soon bedtime arrived and kerosene lamps were lit as the evening ritual wound to a close with children trundled off to the sleeping loft.

My wife's tale is one of continuity, lives unfolding at a gracious pace, lives unlike our modern, highly desired ones with their activities, goals, travel and possessions.

These thoughts stirred within me as Regina and I watched the night encroach upon our yard. Scattered cloud tops are first brilliantly lit by stray rays from the sun beneath the horizon, and then slowly fade as the orangish cast of city lights paints their undersides. The blue of the sky deepens and darkens. Stars emerge and a bat darts across open space between fruit trees. Mosquitoes seek us out, our warm blood their evening meal.

In as much as mobility and wealth have brought us wonders and opportunity, we have lost some simple grace. In the simplicity and stability of their lives, people such as Regina's relatives possess some elements of living that are probably not available to modern lifestyles. I have gained experiences of variety and change; they know the virtues of patience and place. I can almost smell the tobacco.

Afterthoughts

Indigenous cultures believe that all they need shall be provided by God or gods.

And it has been posited that the fall from grace occurred when men and women came to believe the work of the gods to be inadequate.

One day, I told my mentor, Sam, I would like to learn to sit on my back porch and sip iced tea. He chided me, "You'll come up with something to do in five minutes."

In moments of great quiet and clarity, I have seen that I am fueled by a fear deep within me that things are simply not going to be made right. Paralleling that fear is a belief that I must do so. Much of the action that has filled my life, pulling me from a simple state of grace-filled living, has been propelled by these fears and beliefs.

Questions to Consider

How do the activities in my life support or hinder me? Do I enjoy busyness? What is the payoff for my activity choices? What do I value most?

_____
_____
_____
_____
_____
_____
_____
_____

BITTERNESS

SOMEWHERE, at a time and place I cannot recall, I noticed that our elder population contains a great many men and women who have been embittered by life. During my graduate studies in Social Welfare, I heard a great many theories intended to explain the sources of the bitterness. I am not going to pretend that I have a conclusion about the issue, but there is no question that some elders remain vitally alive, thriving and growing. Others collapse in upon themselves into frailty, dependence and discouragement.

About ten years ago, I experienced a vivid and detailed dream of myself. I was old and the courses I had set for my life had crashed around me. I felt an extraordinarily powerful bitterness in me. When I awoke the sense of failure and tragedy lingered, as did a very potent recollection of the dream that is still with me to this day.

The result of the dream was that I became unusually observant of the elders in the community. I experienced an almost magnetic attraction to those who seemed to have made peace with themselves and their lives. Several have become very good friends and I correspond regularly with others. The degree of interest I see myself express toward them surprises me, because I am often too self-absorbed to be very attentive to others. Yet, it is really rather simple…I want what they have. I do not wish to sink into cynicism and bitterness, as I grow older. I know no better way to prevent that than to speak at length and in depth to those elders whose presence and lives seem positive, full and rich.

I suppose my actions are nothing more than reasonable. Our elders have experience, which I lack. They have perspective gained from their own foibles as well as from painful and difficult life lessons. It seems to me that this is the value of our elders - knowledge and experience. And I would like to benefit from it.

Each time I strike up a conversation with an elder, I try to consider what has propelled them to become as they are. The path to satisfaction with my life seems too narrow to discount their experiences. Sometimes, I think they benefit as well.

Afterthoughts

Today, I am profoundly aware of my isolation, painfully so. I wonder if I shall ever break free of the self-centeredness that insists upon excluding others, especially those who have so much experience and knowledge to impart to me. If indeed we are One, then community is holy ground.

Questions to Consider

If in this instant I were to find myself an elder, of what communities would I be a member? What roles would I fill, and from what would my satisfaction come? How can I ensure that bitterness is not my lot?

_____

_____

_____

_____

_____

_____

_____

A CONCRETE BLOCK

IT was an eye-opening experience. Traffic had backed up on a major, cross-town road and I changed lanes to gain some forward progress. As I neared the beginning of the tangle, I saw several cars signaling to change lanes, nice cars driven by nice looking young men. Beyond them sat a working man's pickup from which another young man in jeans and workboots had emerged and walked forward. As I passed I saw a single concrete block had fallen into the road, apparently not from his truck. The man from the pickup arrived at the block and casually tossed it onto the median, then waved the traffic forward.

While it is entirely possible that most of us were simply engaged in productive and active lives, I realized one effect of a society accustomed to affluence and ease - complacency. It is so much easier to change lanes than to remove a concrete block from the road. We need not exit our cushioned, air-conditioned comfort, nor soil our hands or pants. Simply flick the turn signal and go around, leaving the impediment untended and unsolved.

I know at this point I'm supposed to launch into a "good ol' days" lament, chasten some potentially lazy young men, and complain in proper liberal fashion about a lack of action, or in proper conservative tones about the terrible loss of those values which made America strong. It is not as simple as that. Had our younger generations been fired in the crucible of the Great Depression and World War II, they would bear similar values. But that has not been their experience. And frankly, there are more than a few elders who did experience those tribulations who share the complacency, though in different ways.

Wealth and affluence may be their own reward, but they also can bear a bitter harvest.

It would no more occur to someone to move the block, than it would have occurred to my father to waste a dime in 1939. I am so weary of incessant blame. Blame is for victims, pointless and futile. Our problems are not the cause of republicans or democrats, bureaucrats or businessmen, unions, churches, parents, drug addicts, or criminals. "We have met the enemy and it is us," said the wise comic strip character Pogo. And yet we're guilty of nothing more than being lulled to sleep by our isolated, veneered lives. It's pretty and it's posh, but the price of our complacency is steep.

I'm sure there is a solution, but I do not know it. I only know we are slowly sinking into affluence-created hypothermia, drifting off quietly and pleasantly.

A concrete block in the road. I could have stopped and moved it. It didn't occur to me either.

Afterthoughts

Where I do not see, or understand, I do not seem to have access to the power to act.

Questions to Consider

What moments for action escaped me today in my community? How could it be different, and what is the mutual benefit? Is there any act that is not beneficial to others?

_____

_____

_____

_____

_____

_____

_____

_____

PUNKS

IT was a sight I'm sure every adult sooner or later experiences. I was stopped in traffic when I heard the squealing of tires. I glanced in my rear-view mirror as a 1970's era Chevelle approached at breakneck pace before lurching to a stop directly beside me. Through the window I saw four young men. A single word formed on my lips: "punks."

Each man had a cigarette dangling from his lips. Their heads moved jerkily, almost birdlike, as they gestured and pointed. I could imagine their raucous, boisterous voices from the slight bouncing of the car as they moved about. All four had stocking caps pulled down to their eyebrows.

My first thought was one of derision, immediately followed by a question. Do these boys' mothers know how stupid they look? I then realized it was an irrelevant question, no matter how innane their appearance, they likely felt really cool.

I remembered my own adolescent years. While I don't think I was a punk, I'm sure my own non-conforming ways were a source of amusement for my elders. I probably seemed as foolish as did these boys. On more than one occasion, given the extremism of my behavior, adults must surely have uttered the word "punk" about me.

I dismissed my thoughts. The Chevelle roared by as I turned off onto another road. A final glimpse was of one of the young men hanging out the window gesturing at two pretty girls on the sidewalk. The girls giggled in response to his hoots. I laughed at the entire scene, critical thoughts no longer present within me.

The incident slipped away from my memory until later that evening. My seventeen-year-old daughter called home fearfully. A car full of punks had been chasing her and a friend in Natalie's car down a busy road. She had tried to get away to no avail. The punks flashed bright lights, blocked her from exiting, and had tried to run her off the road. Natalie's friend used a cell phone to call the police, and the girls finally broke away to pull into a gas station. The patrol cars were with them, though the punks had escaped. Natalie wanted us to come escort her home.

As my wife, Regina, and I drove across town I related my experience with the Chevelle downtown. We talked at length about abusive behavior that seems endemic in some young men.

There is a strange line between the rowdiness of adolescent behavior and genuinely criminal activity. I do not know where one begins and the other ends. I do not know what ought to be done about it. But I am not surprised that so many people are frightened by the excessiveness of some young men. I'm not surprised the word "punk" springs up so readily to others and me. If I had had the chance, I would have liked to hurt those punks that chased Natalie, conveniently forgetting that I too may have once been a punk.

Afterthoughts

Ugliness is a part of this world, even within me.

Questions to Consider

If the test of life is the acceptance of all things around us as perfect, what is there that I simply cannot or will not accept? Is it possible to muster willingness to relinquish our feelings about it? Why or why not?

_____

_____

_____

_____

_____

_____

_____

_____

IT DOES MATTER

I had an unusual experience which concluded as an affirmation and confirmation. It is sometimes quite pleasant to receive such assurances.

Regina and I were en route to a store at a local shopping center. As we drove onto the property we noticed a broken water line geysering into the parking lot. We entered the store and advised a young woman of the burst pipe. She looked at us rather blankly. We explained in more detail, wasted water, increased common area maintenance fees, and so forth. We then had to tell her she ought to determine how to contact the property manager.

The look in her eyes told me we were greatly inconveniencing her. But I suppose she figured we would be persistent, so she wandered off. When she returned she told us no one knew anything. There was nothing she could or would do.

Regina and I were exasperated, but entered another store. To our dismay we received a very similar response, this time from a young man. He concluded by shrugging, as if to say "not my problem."

I guess we are hard-headed. We tried a third store. This time, though the staff did not know how to proceed, they assured us that the matter was addressed. We were running late so we dashed off. As we drove, Regina and I conferred a bit and concluded that many people are disengaged from the society of their peers. Uninvolved. Disinterested. Conditioned to believe they are not responsible. Perhaps, even that nothing matters.

We are often frustrated by such attitudes. We believe that involvement fosters involvement, that people can make a difference if they will only act. At this particular moment, however, we were dismayed.

On our return home we had to visit the first store, and to our relief the water problem had been solved. As we stood in the store, I felt a tap on my shoulder. I turned and was shocked to see a young woman I had coached in little league softball two years previously. She had been a handful – high-spirited, rebellious, angry. She was also an excellent ball player. When last I had seen her, she had been in some pretty serious trouble with the law. Her future was questionable, it seemed. Now I was delighted to behold the smile upon her face. She told us that she was doing well. She was receiving good grades, was free from troubles with the law, and participated in two sports. Her mother stood beside her and confirmed that all was splendid.

It was a sweet few moments. She agreed to help me coach this year if possible. In several small ways, I heard her gratitude resounding. I was pleased by the encounter.

Later that day, I reflected upon her. I recalled the last words I'd spoken to her two years before as she began All-Star softball. "Listen," I said, "you are an outstanding ball player. Just don't push the system so hard, for better or worse, coaches and umpires have the power. You don't have to live with it, but if you wish to play you have to comply. Don't mess it up girl, I know you can do it."

The memory renewed me; though I will never know what role I played in her life. Our actions do make a difference. In spite of discouraging examples to the contrary, things do matter. Thanks Jahnelle, my life just bore fruit richly.

Afterthoughts

Every now and again, I have had the opportunity to see the effects of my life on others. While some of these cause me to shudder when I become aware of how horribly I can behave, a few confirm an idea that my beloved friend Patrick long espoused – we never know how we might affect others and some of our best moments will come when we are oblivious.

Questions to Consider

With fearless honesty, how have I affected others around me? What is the truth of me in my communities? Can I see myself clearly? Can anyone?

_____

_____

_____

_____

_____

_____

_____

JENNIFER

AS I drove home in the middle of the afternoon, I had a most disquieting experience. A former friend of our eldest daughter, now fourteen, stumbled across a road by our home, falling down drunk, propped up between two young men on either side of her. As my daughter and I passed her, she hollered "Hey, I love you!" then, she laughed uproariously, head back, mouth agape, as only a drunken person could.

She is not a bad kid, but that is virtually true of all young people. My wife and I could see this coming two years ago in her demeanor and actions. Foreshadowing of adolescent troubles to come, she displayed the classic signs of dropping grades and reduced interest. We even discussed it with her one day, at least to the degree one can when the other participant is an adolescent who believes themselves to be invincible. Or worse still, a preteen who has been raised in an alcoholic home and has heard all the lectures since elementary school in drug awareness classes.

It is possible we have desensitized young people with all our fear-based programs and talk on the evils of drugs, sex, gangs, guns, alcohol, and strangers. This would explain the rising incidence of drug, alcohol, and tobacco use. After all, most after school activities contain these admonishments. For those who are prone to such problems, the attempt to educate may do nothing more than heighten their awareness of the glut of violence, sex, and addictive substances in the world that surrounds them. The "Just Say No!" drug campaign is a perfect example. It became a cliché while having no real impact on those most prone to substance abuse problems. They simply joked about it, or ignored it.

Nonetheless, seeing this girl drunk transported me back to my own adolescence: that first whiskey choked down, cigarettes filched and smoked furtively in the storm cellar with the girl next door, and the first time I got drunk, giddy and buoyant before vomiting into shrubbery at my friend's house. The thrill of newly discovered independence, partaking of privileges restricted to adults, heady stuff to any kid coming of age.

I am simultaneously reminded of a recent night at a local shopping center. As two hundred teens under the age of sixteen hung out waiting for movies, several police cars patrolled by, shining lights into dark corners and parked cars. It was a grim reminder of the increasingly hazardous world into which they have been thrust.

Still, hasn't adolescence always been a tumultuous and precarious passage? Several of my friends didn't make it: two suicides, a drug overdose, and a fatal car accident. Is it possible our parental adult anxieties add to the problem? Especially the increasing desire for risk free living with all outcomes controlled and culprits identified? Perhaps some things defy solutions.

Of course, I am troubled by the sight of my daughter's friend, dead drunk at four o'clock in the afternoon. If she blossoms into an alcoholic or addict, her prognosis is quite dismal, misery and tragedy culminating in insanity, incarceration, or even death. Few escape once enslaved. Even those who stay functional, holding their lives together, tend to weave a web of deceit and dismay.

What can we really do for her or those like her? Many of us try to provide places, activities, and education. Ultimately much of our life learning can only take place when the student is willing. Often, it is only pain and failure that can create a fertile ground.

Jennifer is a good kid. I hope she gets hammered by life, and soon. It may be her only hope.

Afterthoughts

Every path is sacred. Despite the reminiscent ache of my own emotionally tortured youth, I can see loveliness in Jennifer and her walk. It is a faint glimmer of a walk in beauty that is not what it seems.

Questions to Consider

How do we view children and youth in my community? Can we see beyond the falseness of media accounts of youth discontent and trouble? Are the so-called "terrible twos" anything other than perfect childhood development? How might I again see young people with awe-filled eyes?

DISFIGUREMENT

I had been working with a disabled man. One side of Dave's face was twisted and sunken. He spoke with some difficulty, and was hard of hearing despite hearing aids. I do not know the tale of his disability, whether injury, disease, or birth complications caused his circumstances. But I wish to recount the story of his presence here in Albuquerque.

My manager told me he was bringing in a man to help us out with some administrative overload, but it was to be a bit unusual. The man was disabled, and despite a graduate degree and solid references, he was unable to find employment. "His face is caved in," he told me, "and no one will hire him because of it." This would be a trial period to see if we couldn't work something out.

I remember the slight queasiness deep in my abdomen as he told me. I have always felt squeamish with disfigurement. I also recall making a mental note to treat him the same as I would anyone.

When Dave arrived for work on his first day, my gut reaction returned as I heard his voice before meeting him. Then introductions, and I felt a firm handshake. I made it a point to look him in the eyes, to see past his disfigurement. He glanced away, as I note he often does in what must be a conditioned response to avoid the look in the eyes of others. Frankly, his malady was not so grotesque as I feared, really quite unremarkable. And as we worked together I learned to speak more loudly and clearly and to face him so he could read my lips.

Very quickly it became quite apparent that Dave had excellent work ability and skills. He was diligent and thorough, as well as willing to pitch in whenever and however he was needed. He was a model employee.

Dave needs neither sympathy, nor compassion. He and his skills stand on their own substantial merits. Most employers would feel fortunate to have such motivation and skills at their disposal. Nonetheless I am distressed over the state of a society, which will not employ someone such as Dave because of physical appearances. In our supposedly enlightened times, I am amazed someone of his skills should be found lacking and remain unemployed for years. Apparently the social effects of Civil Rights, The Americans with Disabilities Act, sensitivity and human diversity training, and the moral teachings of thousands of religious groups have yet to overcome petty human prejudice.

I do not know if Dave's situation will work out here. Despite progressive management and good intentions, the world in which we work and live is quite uncomfortable with physical deformity. Appearance may in fact mean nothing, but it remains the standard that is applied.

Call me naïve. Though we've come so very far, I thought we had come further. Dave's twisted features are a disquieting reminder; there is work yet to be done.

Afterthoughts

I remember a visit to an ashram many years ago. I encountered a woman with terrible scarring from burns and averted my eyes. Someone told me she had been granted an asylum of sorts, a safe haven from prying eyes and insensitive questions.

On another occasion, I interviewed a man with a grotesque facial growth. He told me that his was an outer manifestation of the inner ugliness common to every man and woman.

In the best of moments I can see with an enlightened eye and imagine nothing but loveliness.

Questions to Consider

Where do I feel disfigured? Does this make me less than others? How do others likely view this? What obstacles might this present to the experience of community?

_____
_____
_____
_____
_____
_____
_____
_____

CHILDREN DANCING

IT was a clear, crisp winter's afternoon, though not too cold. I leaned back in my chair and stretched, and then gazed out the large, double windows to the playground amid a circle of buildings that made up the domestic violence shelter where I worked. A fragile, blue sky hung over two little girls playing. They were framed as if in a portrait by the graceful trunks of two leafless, white ash trees. In the background their mothers sat at a concrete picnic table smoking and drinking coffee.

The girls bounced as if on pogo sticks, propelled only by the tireless pumping of their legs. I studied one girl as she knelt. She wore a blue plaid jumper and her light brown hair swept in waves over her shoulders, reddish highlights glinting in the sun. I imagined I could see brilliant blue eyes and pale freckles upon her light skin. Suddenly, she uncoiled like a tightly wound spring, leaping upward and hurling a stick into the air. I heard a faint, shrill shriek as the women turned to watch and her playmate stood with eyes cast upward. The second girl was Hispanic with hair the blue-black color of a raven, braided down her back. A red ribbon bound her hair and stood out against black jeans and a gray pullover. Her teeth sparkled in a broad, open-mouthed smile.

An instant later, the stick fell to the ground. The girls grabbed hands and began to dance a mad, unrehearsed jig. I began to hear their laughter through the walls as they stomped their feet with unfettered joy. I noticed the Caucasian woman repeatedly glance toward the girls. A disapproving look seemed to grow upon her face. Obviously, the raucous play distracted her from her conversation. I could sense tension growing.

The children began to spin with arms straight and elbows locked. Dirt flew from beneath their feet while their hair whipped out in defiance of gravity, the red ribbon like a rapidly rotating beacon. They spun faster still and the little girl in blue laid back her head and let loose a screech that rang brightly in the air. A moment later they collapsed into a heap upon the ground, writhing to rhythmic gales of laughter. Simultaneously, the annoyed mother shot to her feet. I could not hear her words but the snarl upon her face told the tale of the irritation spewing forth.

The girls lay stalk still with their attention riveted to the woman. The atmosphere was pregnant; I hoped the mother would laugh or approach the now frightened girls. But, she launched into a tirade with renewed vigor and righteous indignation.

I sensed the sky dulling. The ash trees seemed to tremble and diminish.

The mother's eyes were dark as she swept her arm in a forceful gesture for the girls to go inside. The girl with the ribbon in her hair began to cry. Her friend glowered stoically, arms crossed and feet planted firmly. The woman's rage grew in response to the defiance. Perhaps she also lamented the child weeping. She gestured again and took a menacing step toward the children. Her head snapped viciously as more words assailed them. This time, the girls flew from her anger and disappeared into a cottage.

The mother gazed after them for an extended moment. She sagged slightly, gathered a deep breath, and returned to the table. Lighting another cigarette, she resumed her conversation.

The space within the ash trees was now motionless and unanimated. I imagined the girls playing happily indoors; but I could not maintain the image. I looked to my paperwork as a sigh escaped. I glanced hopefully through the windows one last time.

It is said we must become like little children to enter the kingdom of heaven. I rued the spoiling of paradise and the memory of children dancing.

Afterthoughts

In a professional development class years ago, we were asked to write on a note card the age at which we believed middle age occurred. I was in my early twenties and imagined it to begin at thirty-five. Curiously, everyone estimated it to be in the future because no one felt old inside. Without fail this reminds me that there is a part of me that never ages, that can still dance, and that will often feel bruised by the seeming senselessness of life.

Questions to Consider

Am I aware of the child within me? How is it expressed, and how is it denied? How do I then express it in the community?

_____
_____
_____
_____
_____
_____
_____
_____

CHARACTERS COUNT

ON a cruise up into the Northeast Heights of Albuquerque, I happened to see a large billboard advertising Character Counts, the school based program meant to develop character in young people. In large looming letters it announced: RESPECT, CARING, TRUSTWORTHINESS, RESPONSIBILITY, CITIZENSHIP, FAIRNESS.

I doubt that anyone would question the value of those six traits. And yet I was aware that one aspect of the program is wrong. We often believe that the provision of information is sufficient to teach. But preaching never changed anyone – never – though we do like it. It is not just the content that is important but the method by which such traits become relevant.

I refer to the people who model and teach those six traits. Parents. Extended family. Teachers. Elected officials. Police officers. Coaches. Mentors. Celebrities. Neighbors. Generally any adult who influences young people.

After all it's great to preach about respect, but what do we learn from the antics of celebrated sports figures who behave terribly? Hardly respect. What of citizenship? What message does a child receive when their parents do not vote and do not take part in community efforts? What do you suppose a child perceives about trustworthiness as he watches the behavior of elected officials or business leaders who are hardly good role models for trust?

Obviously, the point is that words don't teach, behavior does. We are the product of the actions of others, students of our life role models. For example I can tell you that what I learned of citizenship came especially from my father, and most of what I learned of responsibility came from my mother. A football coach and several teachers showed me what it meant to be fair. Respect came from a neighborhood parent, Mrs. Louise Farrell. I learned to care by the actions of my Uncle Norman and Uncle Bob, my dad's friend Joe Tudor, and two adult mentors, Patrick Kurp and Sam Dement.

Perhaps it is not children who need to be taught about character, rather it is adults. Children simply model what they see. Change the behavior of adults and the character of most youth will follow suit.

Let's call it *Characters* Count. Let's emphasize the role we characters play in the formation of character in youth. By adding the characters to the character, we have a surefire formula for success.

Afterthoughts

I wonder about my character, given that I am at times prone to dogmatism and preaching. The very preaching I know to be ineffective creeps into my words and demeanor. While the nature of human behavior guarantees flaws and inconsistencies in me and others, these transform character into characters. And thank God for all those quirky people who have played a part in making us as we are.

Questions to Consider

How can any of us hope to escape our own character flaws? If we should succeed in relief from those limitations, if we should add character, do we become less of the characters from whom others can learn?

_____
_____
_____
_____
_____
_____
_____
_____

DISTANT FIRE

MY wife, Regina, and I were spending our first Thanksgiving alone since our marriage. Natalie and Brianne were with their father in Chicago, offering us a brief respite from the rigors of building our family. After a fine meal we decided to hike with our dogs on the West Mesa, an isolated plateau beyond the city limits. We drove to the northern reaches of the escarpment that snakes along the mesa and entered a deep arroyo lined by gray-black basalt.

We walked amid boulders warmed by the sun, the dogs cavorting amid rocky crags, sandy basins and clump grasses. The day was rich and serene beneath pristine turquoise skies and a faint breeze.

At the end of the arroyo, we exited onto the open mesa. The wind chilled us as we turned to follow a jeep track back to our truck.

A few moments later a strange noise whirred overhead. I shrugged it away, concluding it to be some insect invigorated by the warmth. After a few more steps the noise recurred twice in rapid succession, followed by the unmistakable crack of a rifle.

I spun in the sand toward Regina and barked tersely, "Gunfire!" I dove for her hand and the earth. My heart raced. The dogs yapped at the unseen threat. Paradise crashed in a single, frozen moment.

More shots rocketed by from beyond a low brow of rock that concealed us. We plotted quickly. Regina held the dogs tightly to the ground as I made a mad dash toward a ridge of basalt, which would allow me to flank the gunmen. Another shot buzzed overhead. I shouted several times then stripped off my red jacket, rolled onto my back and desperately threw it into the air. Gunfire echoed anew. I scrambled back to Regina. We crept through sagebrush to the arroyo.

Anger swept over us as we caught our breath in the rocky sanctuary. Rifle fire continued in the distance. We resolved to retreat, drive around from the north, and confront the gunmen. Briskly we marched down the arroyo fueled by indignation and a concern that others might be injured. I worried secretly about confrontation.

The truck sped over the rough terrain, but when we arrived they were gone. Large caliber shell casings and shattered beer bottles littered the ground.

I studied the contour of the land. They had mounted bottles along the brow beyond which we had walked, firing their rifles into open space. A mere hundred yards below our vantage, I spied the spot where we had crumpled to the ground.

The episode shattered our idyllic holiday. Gratitude seemed so much easier before we felt threatened.

Afterthoughts

I love the explanation of insecurity given to me by one mentor. Insecurity is when reality does not conform to my beliefs. I feel secure when my belief system is not threatened. That should be no surprise since my beliefs are the foundation upon which my life is constructed. It is damned uncomfortable to feel insecure, but even more so to question my beliefs.

Questions to Consider

When have I felt insecure? When did I last come to question a belief? What experience brought it about? How did it feel? What was the outcome?

_____
_____
_____
_____
_____
_____
_____
_____

REFUGE

I'VE always been intrigued by how visions can influence us. By vision I mean that inner sense of how something could be…the picture, feeling, or story in our heads that brings forth our passion and motivation.

For the longest time I have had a vision of Albuquerque that I've been hesitant to share, perhaps fearful that it might sound foolish or hopelessly idealistic. But I recently read a short newspaper item about a Great Dane that was burned alive by someone. As usual, the story brought tears to my eyes, followed immediately by the unvoiced vision I've been carrying about with me. And I imagined it was time to give it a voice.

The only word that comes to mind is "refuge." Refuge Albuquerque…an uncommonly humane city that is not afraid to chart a path of compassion. A place of unusual consideration for animals, immigrants, the homeless, children and youth. A community that values diversity, the elderly, the arts and the environment.

I watch as our politicians, and seemingly most of the populace, continue an incessant clamor for Albuquerque to be like other cities. I shudder. It seems to me that many of us are in Albuquerque and New Mexico precisely because it is not like other places. Yet I am aware it is so difficult to create something new rather than emulating that which already exists. It's hard following a road less traveled.

Still a vision of Refuge Albuquerque captures my attention. Imagine a place with a common goal of building a culture of sensitivity and compassion…a city that sets aside common and petty bickering in pursuit of a higher calling. Imagine a community where not one useful and healthy animal is euthanized, where immigrants and the homeless are somehow usefully incorporated, where no child or elder is set aside and forgotten and every expression of humanity is valued, and where the arts, culture and the environment are elevated to share the importance of good economics and democracy.

The picture in my head for Albuquerque is of a refuge from all that is sordid and wearying about the world. And while I do not know the particulars of how we might create such a refuge, I've done so much work with visioning, that I know a vision will carry the day. All we need do is set a standard to guide us.

Refuge Albuquerque! I may be a fool, but why settle for less than the ideal?

Afterthoughts

Refuge is a hopeful ideal that commands a part of me. It is also utopian, and I am prone to seeing such ideals as a preferred state of humanity.

Yet, I wish never to forget that we are surrounded by a community of glory and grace, if we can simply come to see it. There is wonder in all things, perhaps the faint radiance of the Spirit that animates everything that exists.

This then is community for me. A chance to see the extraordinary presence of God, which at best can be a mirror to my own equal holiness.

Questions to Consider

What vision do I carry for my community? What role do I play in its creation?

_____

_____

_____

_____

_____

_____

_____

_____

SONG OF THE WEST MESA

TO the west of the city of Albuquerque, above a jagged escarpment of ancient basalt boulders, lies a high, windswept desert known as the West Mesa. A line of dormant volcanic cones forms a ridge running from north to south atop the mesa from which one can view distant mountain ranges, an infinite turquoise sky, desert stretching westward to the horizon and the fertile, green valley of the Rio Grande which unfurls like a ribbon across the vast, brownish terrain.

The mesa and escarpment were formed millions of years ago when the volcanoes spewed molten rock from the bowels of the earth. Over the ensuing millennia, wind, rain, heat and snow have shaped and softened the landscape. The volcanoes are merely crumbled relics. Powdery silt buries most of the rock though crags and knobs of cinders yet protrude. Hardy sage, yucca and cactus have taken to the soil. Drought stunted juniper and cedar trees dot a land predominated by Indian rice grass and snakeweed.

Arid country creatures lurk amid this rugged terrain. Rattlesnakes and desert mice burrow deeply, typically appearing only in an absence of direct sunlight. Jackrabbits are abundant while mounded cities of prairie dogs occupy far-flung hills. Coyotes prowl as raptors silently and gracefully dominate the heights.

The winding escarpment, the volcanoes and the southern end of the plateau of the mesa form the recently created Petroglyph National Monument which takes its name from the wealth of native etchings carved into rock faces. Encircling the monument are thousands of acres of open space, some of which have been protected by local government. The balance of the land is used primarily for grazing.

This West Mesa is a step-child. Visitors and tourists climb the volcanoes and study the renderings on the basalt, then pass on to more noteworthy attractions: Santa Fe, Mesa Verde, White Sands, Carlsbad and Bandelier. The allure of casino gambling, tram rides, skiing and factory outlet malls also capture the attention of many.

For the most part the mesa is ignored because of its lack. The West Mesa is a hopelessly common place without profound mystery, extraordinary beauty or great entertainment, and certainly without an obvious presence. It is kin to all that is ordinary and is overlooked because humans are drawn to presence rather than absence.

Still, average places comprise the majority of the world. Mystics throughout the ages have sought absence as a destination, whether desert, plains or shore. It is no surprise that Jesus spent his forty days and forty nights in the desert in preparation and purification. While it is the last thing most of us seek, it is absence that nurtures us.

I have only come to understand this in the years I have hiked the mesa. It has become my teacher, confidante, lover and minister. My spirit has been sustained as I have trekked through it, for at the heart of the West Mesa is the essence of all that is. Call it what you wish, but it is that elusive essence which seems beyond mortal expression.

While I lack the ability to readily articulate it, I have felt that essence in my belly. My feet have touched it with each stride. I have sensed its energy as it pulsed in the palms of my hands. And with these experiences I have acquired stories to tell. It is ultimately these which speak, not I, for they are not mine to claim.

I stood in rapture as a western meadowlark sang to the breaking day, one chilly morning, as the sun rose above the Sandia Mountains. My eyes were closed, allowing the melody to pierce my consciousness. Eternity echoed in the tones.

On other occasions I have felt transported from my body. I saw with new eyes the auras of the rock, earth and plants. I felt the flow of life coursing steadily through the mesa. Monstrous spring winds have blown me before them. The setting sun has glimmered on gently swaying clumps of grass and made sunflowers radiant in a fragile atmosphere. I have watched great slashes in the soil filled by the inexorable accumulation of a billion grains of sand.

Often I have taken troubles to the West Mesa where they have been intensified and reflected upon until I could neither escape nor repress them. Mercilessly they have been drawn forth by the vast and quiet desert. When my despair erupts it is absorbed patiently and endlessly by the same emptiness that surrounds me. It seems the mesa's ability to wash away my emotions is inexhaustible. I am held in the bosom of this essence and relieved of my heartache.

I remember the day my mother died. It was one of many times I have taken a burden of grief to the mesa. I numbly walked several miles, directionless. Then in an arroyo I constructed a memorial for my mother from sage and rock. An overwhelming pain surfaced just as I finished and I collapsed into the sand and wept. I thought I might die from the fury of the hurt I felt, but in the end I lay exhausted and spent. For a time I was comforted.

On a curve on a vacant asphalt road leading to a dead end in the heart of the West Mesa stands a small white cross. A young woman died there. The ground, already holy in its own right, now holds her memorial and a sacred memory of her.

There is a richness to the mesa which defies words. In absence, life pushes forth with exceptional fervor. I have seen a verdant garden in this desolation, which is built upon life, death and the spirit that binds all things.

My experiences have taught me a new perspective. There are awe inspiring natural places which provoke us and urge us to peer beyond our petty selves. They batter us into an awakening. And there are common spaces, like the West Mesa, which predominate our world. In them we are refined and purified, learning to see beauty, rhythm and meaning in the simplest of settings.

If there is a single message of the West Mesa, it is oneness. We are not apart; there is no separation. Spirit dwells in you in as much as it dwells in me, in the mighty as well as the meek, the beautiful as well as the seemingly vile. It is a message of reverence for all things, recognition of a common bond within all. We cannot isolate any single thing as sacred or apart. Either the Essence is in everything or it is in nothing. If we would revere one place or one creature, we must revere all places and all creatures.

I have felt a vibrant spirit in the asphalt before city hall and seen an aura emanating from a brick building. Meadowlarks sing within the city, and the trees in my backyard glow in the morning light.

The natural places we deem extraordinary must be points of departure from which we bring new reverence to every facet of our lives. They cannot and must not be safe havens to which we cling or within which we hide. Reverence will restore us and everything around us, but if we insist on limiting the boundaries of our reverence to pristine settings they will perish with us.

We clamor to save the last of the wild places, thinking humanity to be their salvation. I have seen a more poignant reality: that the wild places are our salvation. We must learn from them and apply our knowledge beyond them.

This is the message we must carry into our cities, our neighborhoods, our families and our lives. If we cannot yet see the holiness in concrete and masses of humanity, we have not yet seen the truth. The spirit of the mesa must live in all things. Either God is everything, or God is nothing. The West Mesa has shown me.

Afterthoughts

    I distinctly remember the first time I saw an aura surrounding an outcropping of rock on the West Mesa. It was some months later that I saw that same haloing around a structure in downtown Albuquerque.

    It remained hard for me to believe I was seeing Spirit, because I am inherently skeptical. Then I remembered a good friend, a professed agnostic, who prays regularly. When I pointed out this inconsistency to him, he laughed at me, and then said, "I don't know about God, but I do have experience that it works."

Questions to Consider

    What have I experienced? How does this contrast with what I believe? What proof do I have of my beliefs that is not grounded in personal experience?

_____

_____

_____

_____

_____

_____

_____

_____

PERSONALLY AND PRIVATELY

WHO AM I?

I have a name, but who am I? Am I not the story of a life that's been lived? And hasn't my identity shifted, as have my circumstances?

When I was a boy, named after my father, I was referred to as Ron Jr. or Little Ron. That's how I was perceived. I was never more aware of that perception than when I visited my Aunt Frances and Uncle Bob for the first time since I was a teenager. Frances hugged me and announced to my uncle, "Bob! Look how big Little Ron is!" Then she looked at me and said, "You've really grown!" Once I was a male child named Little Ron, perhaps a smaller version of my Dad, perhaps not.

As I grew my identity changed. As a native of Oklahoma, I was soon tagged with the omnipresent –y. Ronny. Just like Bobby, Billy, Danny, Joey, Jimmy, and so forth. You know you're from the south central part of the country when you've been y-ed. So my name, Ronny, identified me as an Oklahoma boy. And at one point in high school I was similarly tagged as Ron Bob. We all know that everyone from Texas and Oklahoma has a middle name of Bob or Ray and Ron Bob sounded a little more plausible that Ron Ray. So my name marked me as an Oklahoman.

It was in high school that I came by another nickname. This one came about as a result of my accomplishments on the football field, where I was pretty ferocious. My peers began to refer to me as "Big Ron." The pointing of a finger with the hand molded to the shape of a gun is quite important to this particular name. It was comparable to what one might have said a decade ago, "You're the man!" So for a time, I was "Big Ron."

Then came college and a nickname, which in retrospect, is a bit embarrassing. (Whoever coined that word, embarrass, really knew what they were implying…em-bare-ass.) At that time it was important to have a name in the fraternity to which I belonged. So I christened myself "Ron Bacardi" after the well-known liquor. It seemed like a good idea at the time.

When I graduated from college I went to work for General Electric Company and I became RD. That was really none of my doing. Like many large organizations, use of the first two initials made oneself identifiable from others. It may also have been a bit pretentious. So RD marked me as a corporate man, a young executive, and perhaps a player in my own mind.

It wasn't long though before my peers at work discovered the competitive part of my personality. It readily emerged in my job performance as well as leisure activities such as volleyball and golf. I can be intense and highly motivated. One day as we performed an inventory of large crates of products it was necessary to do a fair amount of climbing around atop them to get proper counts. A female fellow employee who was paired with me watched as I vaulted about thirty feet off the ground. It was the era of Sylvester Stallone and I was soon christened Ronbo after Stallone's ultra bad character Rambo. Ronbo. Now that tells you a lot about me, doesn't it?

In adulthood I have actually seen the reemergence of a childhood name – Ronnie, though now spelled "ie" rather than "y." Only a few male friends use it. It no longer denotes my geographic heritage; rather it is a term of endearment from the best of friends. I suppose that is a mark of a coming of age. I'm finally old enough to participate in intimate male relationships without it being perceived as unmanly. So, to a few I am Ronnie.

More recently, a female friend gave me another nickname. She had come to know me in a spiritual environment and was taken by what she called "my presence." She said that there was a lot to me. Since this occurred in New Mexico, she took the Spanish word for "more' and tacked it on. I became Ronniemas.

I was touched. And truth be known, my ego was a bit inflated by her observations. I'm a typical guy, after all, and always happy to impress women.

It was then that clarity, and perhaps a bit of humility, descended upon me. The English translation of Ronniemas would be "more Ron." MoRon. Moron. When I took to signing some of my e-mails to family and friends with MoRon, I found some of them insulted on my behalf. Even after explaining it, they still found it demeaning. Insulting or not, it is now a part of me as well.

Then followed another nickname of praise. A man I mentor told me one day he had renamed me: The Ronnie Lama! Ha! Imagine that. Once again I was pleased, until I shared the tale with a woman friend who laughed far longer than seemed appropriate. Yet now I am The Ronnie Lama too.

Who am I? Probably I am as circumstances dictate, many things to many people.

I imagine a day will come when my children will name me as a grandfather. It is also likely that my grandchildren will mispronounce it, just as my nieces and nephews once knew me as Unca On. And I shall be pleased to answer, no matter the name.

A final question is compelling. If I am not these, or if I am all of them, then who is the one who plays these roles and takes on these identities?

There must be more to me than meets the eyes, or even the names.

Afterthoughts

Central to my life has been a quest for meaning and purpose. And central to that is the identity of the self. I am aware of always having sought to be relevant, though I would be hard pressed to explain the quest.

I have come to prefer seeing my life in the context of roles, none of which is really me. Within it all, I imagine a great and glorious identity for each of us, an identity that is not a name, a role, or even a personality, but a perfect and holy expression.

Questions to Consider

What roles do I have for myself? Am I these? If not, who do I imagine myself to be? If so, have I chosen the roles, or they me?

_____

_____

_____

_____

_____

_____

_____

_____

DESPAIR AND TEA

I awoke to despair the other day. It is not that uncommon and not a particularly big deal. But I am always puzzled by its occurrence because I do not know its source. This is the first time I have attempted to give voice to it, at least in a public medium.

Mostly, the cause seems to be disappointment. I have not succeeded as I thought I should. I have been unable to attain the socially desired norms of a svelte body, classic wit, and exceptional success. I argue with my wife and daughters more than is good or useful to them or myself. I am dogged by feelings that I just cannot get it together. And in the face of social values that suggest I ought to know what I am doing and where I am going, I do not know. In fact I feel quite directionless at times. And confused. The world is so fragmented and broken. My efforts at compassion and improvement seem futile. Yet I must awake each day, muster my good will, a sense of humor, and desire to invest some effort, then slog into the world of which I am part.

Psychiatrists might diagnose me as depressed and recommend medication. Many people take such mood altering substances regularly. Millions of others seek relief with alcohol, illegal drugs, and a wide range of compulsive behaviors. But I have been told my feelings are simply a part of life. One friend calls it "divine discontent." Another regularly reminds me "this too shall pass," which actually applies to everything, that which we call good *and* that which we call bad. It's all temporary.

The thoughts themselves sounded terribly depressing. A voice in my head muttered, "Lighten up man."

Still, there is comfort in admitting that some days the weight of the world and my life are too much. I am too heavy, too serious, too burdened, too troubled. And most significantly of all, I don't know why. For that matter, I don't know who or what to blame. And sometimes, positive thinking looks like just another mood altering substance.

As I walked into the business where I worked I recalled Wim Wender's movie about angels, "Wings of Desire." Specifically I remembered an angel named Willie listening to Peter Falk, who plays himself in the movie. Falk is a former angel who chose to become mortal and he can sense Willie's presence. Falk joyfully and poignantly describes the wonderful and simple pleasures of being mortal, like the smell, touch, and taste of a steaming cup of coffee on a cold day.

I stood in the parking lot and became attentive. I felt the refreshing cold air on my face. Slowly and carefully, I inhaled the morning air. It was delicious with the faint hint of the odor of the earth and the dampness of the dew. When I entered the building I poured myself a cup of herbal tea, then wrapped my hands around the mug to feel the warmth. I sniffed gently at the subtle aroma of chamomile. Taking a sip, I savored the heat and texture of the liquid.

Then the thought came to me, "I am so thankful for life."

More thoughts followed. "I do not know what hurts. I do not know what ought to be done about it. But, this too is good."

Tears welled in my eyes and a sadness in my belly. I sipped more tea.

Life is good. Paradise perhaps. But not all is perfect, even in Eden. There is trudging to be done, tears to be wept, and laughter to be found.

Afterthoughts

Some years ago I was fond of saying, "Another day in paradise…it just doesn't look like what I expected."

Thank goodness for gifts, sometimes in unusual form, which shake me out of the seemingly inevitable funks of life. Still, I know the real solution is to embrace the depression, to make peace with it, to adore it.

Questions to Consider

Can I embrace a funky mood? Or do I seek only to find an exit from it? Why or why not?

_____

_____

_____

_____

_____

_____

_____

_____

FREEDOM

IN 1988 I left a career under duress. Personal problems including a painful divorce from my first wife Melanie forced an overhaul of my priorities and perspectives.

It was a traumatic time despite a generous severance package. The record of my accomplishments and promotions translated into a substantial windfall. Still, it hurt.

An encounter with an acquaintance brought to light one of the most significant sources of my discomfort. He wanted to know of my plans, but I honestly could not say. I was single, debt-free, and uncommitted. With the severance benefits, I was funded for a number of months. I needed some time.

He responded, "It must be nice to be so free."

His response triggered inner turmoil, which took a few days to find the words to express. I had spent my life living the aspirations of others: parents, coaches, managers, and companies. Freedom meant I must find my own way. What do I wish to be or do? Where would I like to go? What do I value?

I had no answers to these questions. I was thirty-one years old and had not the slightest idea of my hopes, dreams, and loves. It had been so easy to do another's bidding. No wonder I was disquieted.

In ensuing years I have pursued elusive answers. In the meantime I have remarried, become a parent, acquired possessions, and incurred debt. I have worked in several fields and completed a master's program. Counseling has been essential, and more extensive than I am comfortable admitting.

Chagrined, I must admit that I am a work in progress; I have few answers. But I am not alone. I understand, contrary to prevailing social myths, that most of us will only understand our lives in retrospect. If we are fortunate and wise we may succeed in dredging clarity out of the past that blurs behind us.

Still, I have found an activity for which I have passion. It is giving voice to the thoughts within me, through essays such as this as well as before audiences. It is genuinely fun, though not a viable livelihood. Perhaps it never shall be.

A very dear friend once told me that I expected too much from jobs, that satisfaction must often come from beyond a career. A job might suffice to allow us to pursue our passion.

In retrospect, he might have been right. But as I spoke to my friend just last week, I asked him if it might be possible to create a livelihood from a passion. "Maybe," he said, "but you must not forget that the most important thing is to have fun."

Finally I saw the answer to my quest. I want to have fun…to play. The details are not particularly important, except as a means to an end. What is fun for others may not be fun for me. What is important is to follow my passion. If I am fortunate, it may someday make sense. Perhaps even be profitable. No matter, at least it will have been enjoyable, and I finally will have been able to be free.

Afterthoughts

    As I reflect, I realize that it may be possible to make a living out of a passion. Perhaps I am on the cusp of just such an occurrence. Perhaps not.

    These thoughts bring me back to the most important question. Am I having fun?

    I honestly don't know, because my vision is so clouded by the brainwashing of my society. But I know I am content. I know that most of the time I would not trade my lot for anything.

Questions to Consider

    What do I wish to be or do? Where would I like to go? What do I value? How do these compare to my current way of being and doing? Am I happy with my lot?

_____
_____
_____
_____
_____
_____
_____
_____

BLACKBERRIES

WHEN I was a boy, many hours would be spent clambering amongst the boulders behind our house, which nurtured huge berry brambles. Purple juice would stain the fingers and faces of me and my siblings as we collected pails of the fruit. Sweating beneath the unrelenting sun and torn by the numerous thorns, we would emerge from our foraging with tired bodies, snarling stomachs, and cuts stinging from salty sweat. Assuming we did not eat too much of the fruits of our labor, mother would fix huge berry cobblers. While she tended to the baking I would plunge myself into a cool shower, washing away the grime and sweat. Then we would gorge ourselves on the hot, sweet, cobbler buried beneath scoops of vanilla ice cream.

In my memory, the berry brambles were a world apart, buffered by rock piles that must have generated the extra heat the blackberries seemed to love. Because they were a natural attraction to kids and creatures alike, for many weeks my life unfolded around them. I remember a rock fight with my brother that ended when a chunk of sandstone I threw slammed into his head just as he peeked from behind a boulder that sheltered him.

It may have been that same summer when gathering berries by myself one day, I looked down at my ankle and screamed at the snake's body I saw wrapped around it. I leaped away and ran as fast as I could. I can still recall my panicked panting as I stood on the back porch, amazed at my unscathed escape, only to look down and see my sock rolled down in the same shape that had frightened me. I felt so foolish I couldn't even laugh at myself.

These memories flooded back to me a few summers ago as I traveled cross-country with my nephew, camping and exploring. We took a break driving through southern Missouri to cool off in the clear, pristine waters of the Current River. After relaxing, I noticed berry brambles laden with the largest blackberries I had ever seen. I filled my belly and a large travel mug with them as a flood of recollections rippled through me. I was absolutely delighted with my find, and, with the marvelous events of my youth, which I had long forgotten.

Buying berries from the store just isn't the same. Something of the hands-on experience adds immeasurable value, though I am unable to identify it exactly. When I speak of these things to Regina, Natalie and Brianne, who know very little of berry brambles, they do not understand. I suppose each of us possesses our own fond memories. For me, it is the blackberries of summer.

Afterthoughts

If there is anything that should amaze us, it is the remarkable potency of memories. Given that they are frozen in a past that is no more, I wonder how much they define me?

This is an important question since the nature of the world and perhaps the universe is a state of flux…evolution…change. I would go so far as to say that God does not exist in a frozen construct. So if my memories are me, then I am perpetually trapped in a past that is not only unreal but unrealized.

Questions to Consider

What memories are most powerful for me? How do they influence me today? Are they valid? Joyful? Painful? How much of me is from my past?

_____

_____

_____

_____

_____

_____

_____

_____

IRRATIONAL AND NORMAL

THERE we were, deep within the heart of the West Mesa, my dogs and I, hiking along. As we crested a rise in the jeep track, I was quite surprised to see a pickup truck in an arroyo and a man furiously discarding home improvement debris. I immediately called my dogs to me and quickly departed. After previous odd encounters, I had no desire to find out if this guy would get weird on me.

As we continued the hike, I was struck by the inconsistency of the man's behavior. The bed of his truck overflowed with the evidence of human industry. Yet there was a kind of spiritual or mental lethargy about his method of waste disposal. On one hand I saw extensive proof of the man's effort with improving his home, and on the other, his obvious disinterest in a comparable display with the construction waste.

I have seen other human inconsistencies which I find curious as well. One day I sat sipping coffee near a local gym. I could only laugh as energetic men and women leapt from their cars after parking in the firelane. The walk across the parking lot, a distance of fifty yards, was apparently too much for these athletically inclined souls who would soon be aerobically walking the treadmill or climbing the stairmaster.

On another occasion, I watched a heavily muscled young man clad in body building attire replete with one of those wide, weightlifting belts exiting the grocery store. He pushed a shopping cart with a single bag in it. I remember how odd it seemed that it would not occur to a body builder to carry a grocery bag. Perhaps he had already maxed out his biceps and triceps for the day.

These observations led me to recall a scientific article I read over ten years ago. The author lamented the irrational behavior of the human race. He also expressed concern, for our entire system of justice and law assumes a rational man. According to rational thought, the possibility of cancer from smoking, AIDS from high risk behavior, or even traffic citations for speeding should discourage such behaviors. Yet, as the author observed, we do whatever we wish, then seek justification for our actions or conclude that we must personally be exempt from logic and the laws of probability. In a nutshell, we have never been logical, rational creatures.

This is the only explanation for the guy who discards limbs and branches along the roadside, then purchases firewood from a vendor on that same road. Or someone such as myself, an aspiring environmentalist, who loves to play golf, arguably one of the most environmentally destructive activities created by man. Or the person who drives aggressively, passing others so fast they can barely glimpse the

Christian fish affixed to his bumper, or the sticker encouraging random acts of kindness. One day I saw a terribly decrepit car parked alongside the road with a sunshade in the window advertising a prestigious university for improving your career. We are at best a paradox, at worst, fools and hypocrites.

When I told a friend these thoughts, he laughed. Then he said, "And what a party we have when we come together!"

That's a comfort to me. I've spent my life trying to appear reasonable, rational, and logical, while failing miserably. As it turns out, it's normal to be irrational. I feel better already.

Afterthoughts

There is a piece of my personality that is zealous, and sometimes nearly fundamentalist. As a result, I am inclined toward passionate and dramatic actions, the proverbial "fool for love" and any other meaningful matters. Especially this has been true with regard to responsible actions and behavior.

I remember reading that our passions hinder the effectiveness of our actions, because they are of the self. The item suggested that when we finally rid ourselves of self-based zeal, which has proven to be no small undertaking for me, then we might act from higher purpose.

Questions to Consider

What passions fuel me? Does it work well for me? Is there a better way?

_____

_____

_____

_____

_____

_____

_____

_____

SOCIAL CAPITALISM

I can't tell you how gratifying it is to finally find a phrase to describe something. I had that experience with a dilemma I've faced for some time. Specifically, I've been trying to find a way to adequately describe my belief system and myself. Now, I know I am a social capitalist.

The notion is a spin on "venture capitalist" but it makes two important distinctions. First, it denotes a primary interest in community, culture and society, the world and people around us. That's captured by the word "social."

Secondly however is the idea of capitalism, which as we understand it, involves private investment and profit making. The investment I make certainly can involve money, but also includes my life and me. I am the investment, which includes my resources. And there is a profit, though it is not limited to monetary yields. It includes quality of life. That's the payoff.

The reason I'm so enamored with this idea of "social capitalism" is simple. It shifts the focus from wealth and power for me, to the world around me. It directly addresses the obvious problems that have emerged throughout our culture with regard to ever growing self-centeredness. Let's face it. Most of the problems in government, communities and business of late, stem from a growing tide of selfishness. We've forgotten that we're in this together, that it's not just about me and mine.

It seems that our form of economic capitalism doesn't understand that the purpose of money, investment, jobs, and so forth is to make a contribution to our society. Instead we've embraced a philosophy of self-enrichment, often at the expense of others, and certainly at the expense of quality of life and our physical world.

So I am proud to say that I am a social capitalist. I invest my life and my resources in my community, culture and society. I invest so we can benefit. I invest because the creation of opportunity and nurturing of new ideas is beneficial for all of us. It creates wealth, health and vitality in which we can all participate.

My mentor, a pragmatic man, would now say, "Ron, those are pretty high-falutin' ideas you're tossing around." And he would be right. But something in me refuses to accept that we cannot be led by the marvelous visions and passions that animate us. And I am delighted to see such potential in this marvelous world that surrounds me.

Afterthoughts

    I cringe as I read the judgment, which I hold for the culture I am a part of. Is it wrong to state the seemingly obvious? No, the wrong resides in my seeing, not in that which surrounds me. Even if the conclusion is valid, the wrongdoing, whether real or imagined, is dangerous to all that I hold dear.

    For me, the hardest lesson is learning to find no wrong. None.

Questions to Consider

    Where am I invested? What activities, people and circumstances? And what does this say of what I value?

_____

_____

_____

_____

_____

_____

_____

_____

RECREATION

I sometimes wonder how it is that our ideas about recreation have evolved from the root "recreate," which means, "to create anew." I am certain that those who coined the English phrase, sometime in history, meant to re-create, refresh, renew, and revitalize. Somewhere between then and now our perception of re-creation has been altered. For many it now represents busyness and activities or expensive undertakings such as boating or camping, sports or travel. How many times have you returned from recreational activities or vacations only to find backlogged chores, overflowing "in" baskets, steep credit card debts, or a weary mind and body?

These thoughts emerged a few years ago when my wife, Regina, and I planned a vacation to the Yucatan peninsula of Mexico. We knew we sought rest and relaxation so we avoided Cozumel and Cancun. By chance, our travel agent stumbled across a brochure for a retreat south of the tourist meccas, a place called Chenchomac. It sounded off the beaten path, so we opted to spend a few days there before going to Isla Mujeras, a tourist destination, but pretty laid back.

Upon arriving in Mexico and after a speedy highway drive to Tulum from Cancun, we traveled a long way on a dirt and sand road that fronted the beach. We were in the hinterlands, heading south past a few resorts frequented by Mexican citizens and a number of local residences.

Chenchomac was unexpectedly remote and rustic, with a sprinkling of one-room bungalows just above high tide, and only a handful of guests. No one spoke English. The electrical generator was turned off at nine o'clock each evening and there were no televisions, radios, or transportation.

The first day, in the absence of distractions, we slept. Really slept. It took a retreat such as this for us to discover how tired we were. Then on day two we slept, made love, slept, walked the beach, played with two local boys, slept, made love, beachcombed, and met the pet javalina, Seraphin. We talked less and less. And on the third day we were renewed. I had not felt so refreshed in years. I had been re-created.

Regina and I vowed we would seek simple vacations, near home, as well as slowing the pace of our lives. We both relished the deep and long lasting sense of rejuvenation and were willing to discard some entertainment and excitement from our lives.

We have been somewhat successful at re-creation since that time. I find we seek to do less in all areas of our lives. Admittedly there are numerous distractions: children, cinema, family, retail stores, and the constant bombardment of advertisement extolling entertainment and activity. It's difficult trying to drop out. I am an adrenaline junkie, but I now know what it feels like to be re-created. And I know how harried my daily life can become.

I told Regina that I have set a new goal for myself. Soon, I would like to be able to take a day or a few hours, whenever I wish and just sit on the back porch with a pitcher of iced tea. I want to relinquish my compulsion to read, renovate the house, pay bills, run errands, do chores, or be entertained: to just sit and let renewal seep into my body from the sun, the air, and the wind. It may not seem productive or exciting, but it sure sounds nice. I love recreation.

Afterthoughts

Well it seemed like a good idea at the time, but more has been revealed. I avoid restive times. An inner compulsion has fueled me all my life...to be active and to be engaged. It is an old idea, some holdover from childish days that suggests that things will not work out unless I am in pursuit of them. Thus I remained busy.

Yet I have made progress on this belief, which no longer serves me so well. And I have found an inclination to stay busy. Why? Because I love it! Because it brings meaning to me! Because it sometimes has great value to me and to others!

The underlying cause has been transformed, but the outer behavior remains quite similar. I am different, but my behavior is not.

Questions to Consider

How do I keep myself distracted? Why? Does it work in my life? Is there a price paid for such busyness? Do I feel guilt when not keeping busy? How can I re-create?

_____
_____
_____
_____
_____
_____
_____
_____

HIDEAWAY TRUTHS

I had a curious and humbling experience. I was literally in mid-sentence explaining to a client group principles applicable to one line of my work, group facilitation, when I suddenly recalled something I had overheard a few weeks before. In an instant, I realized what I was saying wasn't accurate. Now I could have stopped, but that would have been a bit too exposed, so I finished expounding, and defended my perspective though it was now no longer valid.

Fortunately, I did proceed to examine the facts and my position. It was then I fully understood an important principle of human behavior. The greatest obstacle to truth is our own certainty. Whenever I am convinced I've cornered the market on the truth, it is almost certain I am in denial and delusion.

While it's bad enough to be wrong about something and ignorant of my own ignorance, its even worse when I feel compelled to continue to defend my position out of some warped sense of principle. And yet that is precisely what takes place, especially if I am in a position of prominence or power. When is the last time you heard an elected official, a corporate executive, or a celebrity admit they had been mistaken?

It doesn't happen very often, does it? Now that would suggest that either most of us have all the answers, or we're very reluctant to admit when we don't.

Imagine, we live in a culture and world where it is unlikely to hear the truth spoken once it is revealed. Now that's frightening. Think of the implications. How many people in power are deluded and unable to see it or admit it?

One of the most powerful quotes I've ever heard came from Mahatma Gandhi. He said, "I am committed to truth, not consistency." Apparently, Gandhi had realized that his certainties were transitory and subject to change. Perhaps that is part of what made him a revolutionary and humble leader.

One of the most potent practices I've been exposed to came from my mentor. In the wake of my recent self-revelation, I find myself using it frequently now as a reminder. "I do not know what ought to be, nor what may be wrong, nor what should be done about it."

I have opinions that stand in the way of the truth. And that is the truth.

Afterthoughts

What a gloriously curious creature I am: inconsistent, illogical, and deluded.

I recall a notion that we have a standard of human perfection that flies in the face of all we see in the natural world. A head of lettuce may be slightly misshapen, a bit ragged and off color. Yet it is perfectly suited to its purpose, superbly so.

Therein lies the glory of me: imperfect and yet perfectly suited. Could the design possibly be more lovely?

Questions to Consider

What opinions do I intractably hold? Are they true? Can I be sure they are true? How do I behave given these opinions? How might I be if they were found untrue?

_____

_____

_____

_____

_____

_____

_____

BISON

THERE I was, cruising up Interstate 25 through the Pecos country en route to Colorado for a conference. I don't know about others, but oftentimes the vacant open road is an invitation for dormant feelings to emerge. So it was in this instance. Tears welled. And I felt the heaviness of questions about all the losses of my life. Had I failed? Does life ever fulfill all the hopes, dreams, and expectations we all bear?

The country opened up into high plains just south of Las Vegas, New Mexico. The sky loomed, expansive blue from horizon to horizon. I felt my mood lift. I adore high open spaces. Then, just a few miles beyond Las Vegas, I spotted a cluster of antelope grazing, and then another. I noticed wildflowers fluttering in the breeze.

My truck hurtled over a rise in the road. Off to the west, great hairy humps appeared amid the golden, waving grasses beneath the Sangre de Cristo Mountain range.

Bison! I thought with unimaginable delight. I burst into joyful tears. Why? I don't know. Perhaps it was utterly coincidental. Or it may have been a counter reaction to the bout of sadness. Who can say? But I want to believe that it was the presence of those magnificent creatures in their native grasslands. Creatures which were almost exterminated.

If there is ever proof of rebirth, bison are it. They are a message of extraordinary hope in complicated times. I suppose I could draw conclusions about my own rebirth from life difficulties. But it just doesn't seem right to do so. The fact is, sometimes joy just comes. And if those hulking phoenixes can inspire, then so be it.

I grinned until it hurt. Even now as I recount my experience, I feel the elation swell! in my heart. Bison! Beautiful New Mexico! Joy! Need I say more?

Afterthoughts

Life is fired at us from point blank range without warning. It is only an illusion that any plan or expectation will be fulfilled. Perhaps curiosity is the only valid perspective for me. It's certainly obvious that anytime I expect more than the unexpected and unexpectable, it presents nothing but problems.

Questions to Consider

If it is true that the nature of life is utterly spontaneous, how do my actions compare? My emotions? My thoughts?

_____
_____
_____
_____
_____
_____
_____
_____

A GLIMPSE INSIDE

I once read an essay that changed me forever, but first it made me extremely uncomfortable. It revealed a chink in my intellectual and emotional armor. The piece came from an incarcerated man, sentenced to die for the rape and murder of eight women. Unlike the typical jailhouse rant, this account didn't insist on the author's innocence. Neither did it attempt to blame any number of possible culprits. Instead, the convict's words illuminated his circumstances.

Since the onset of puberty he had been subject to powerful and violent images in his mind. These mental pictures were so strong that they seemingly compelled him to perpetrate violence at women. Yet it was only in retrospect that he was able see the power of that compulsion. Once incarcerated and sentenced to die, he began receiving injections of a drug that decreased his body's production of testosterone. The compulsion vanished. It became possible for him to see a woman and not be propelled by the portraits in his mind.

His physicians speculated that for reasons beyond their ability to discern, a perfectly normal hormone rendered him into a creature of violence. While he was certainly guilty of the actions for which he was charged, he was neither evil nor a monster. Instead the chemistry of his body betrayed him. The penalty would be his execution.

Being a fairly logical observer, I saw the reasonableness of his explanation though the skeptical critic within me questioned the validity of his account. Perhaps not coincidentally, circumstances arose in my life that allowed me the opportunity to see a variation on his circumstance.

All my life I have battled overeating. Like most chronic dieters I believed it was a matter of willpower and sufficient self-control, what some would call a moral issue. By that I mean that this world had convinced me that it was a shortcoming in me for which I ought to exercise a measure of self-discipline, restraint and effort.

I discovered a book that suggested that the compulsion to eat was fueled by brain chemistry and that adopting a particular pattern of eating would eliminate that unreasonable drive. I followed the directions. Within twenty-four hours I was able to successfully restrain myself. Over days the problem was removed.

I remained suspicious, yet circumstances soon took me away from the patterned eating. The compulsion returned, as did an inability to resist. I could not not eat.

I returned to the dietary plan and once again the compulsion vanished. I possessed an ability to choose, which formerly had been absent. Freedom from that unseemly drive has remained at bay. To outward appearances I possess willpower, self-control and discipline.

There were other examples with other people. Slowly I became convinced that behaviors which are deemed inappropriate, or evil, by our society, are often the product of body chemistry and genetics. And I stood in awe of this one man's essay, words that banished the notion of evil from my beliefs.

In the closing of his article, the man suggested nothing more than the need to question our assumptions. He offered that if our society could acknowledge those dilemmas, which are not simply explained by laying blame upon personal choice or labeling people evil and their behaviors wrong, we would then begin to seek solutions. Then the harms and tragedies would not be in vain.

I am obliged to carry his message forth. His story changed me, and my beliefs. The result has been the birth of a compassion through which I see others and their actions or inactions.

Modern science and understanding allow an unprecedented opportunity to glimpse within ourselves, to see as none have seen before us. In seeing anew we stand at the cusp of a human transformation, a moment poised to give birth to true compassion for others and ourselves.

Afterthoughts

It hurts my heart to consider the implications of a man destined to die for nothing more than biochemistry run amok. How convenient and comfortable it is when I blindly blame evil and wickedness, or suppose that personal choice and consequences can explain humanity's foibles.

Questions to Consider

Do I believe in evil? If so, who told me? Can I confirm it based on personal experience? Is there any personal evidence to refute the belief? Have I knowingly and willingly chosen the deeds which have resulted in problems for me or others?

_____

_____

_____

_____

_____

_____

_____

_____

AMERICAN PIE

I was standing outside a store a few days ago as muted music wafted toward me, too faint to be sure if I knew the melody. I caught myself leaning forward to listen more carefully, attracted by an unconscious force. Indeed, I knew the music.

In an instant I was transported back to the early seventies, a sultry summer's night as my Volkswagen Bug hurtled through the darkness of the Oklahoma night, toward a rendezvous with drinking buddies at the lake north of my hometown. Humid air rushed through open windows as Don McLean belted out the lyrics to "American Pie."

As I stood on the Albuquerque sidewalk, I was filled with a roar of nostalgia and bittersweet memories that almost brought tears to my eyes. I could taste the Coors beer, a favorite at that time at teen-aged Oklahoma parties. The scent of the night air, the warmth of the wind and the sound of lapping water at shore's edge came gently to me, as did thoughts of my friends Randy Hall and Hal Lackey laughing uproariously at some humorous tale.

Then came the rich recollection of lovely, lissome young women. Bobbie Jo Faulkenberry. Rita Anderson. Audie Ward. Fictitious dates and flings flooded through me, hormonal entanglements all.

I remembered how it feels to be potent and passionate, to dream, to see without limit, and to feel unbridled joy.

A truck blasting down the street brought me back with a start. "American Pie" faded. The reverie broke and I returned to the world. The demands of the day lay before me, the challenges of work, daughters, and responsibilities.

I was aware of the burden of my life, and in that, the nostalgic allure of the carefree summer days of my youth. But I noticed a lightness within me. The zealous passion of youth is never really lost. Certainly it is obscured by years, by duties real and imagined, and by countless disappointments. But it still lives in me. Thank goodness for moments that reawaken and renew us.

Afterthoughts

God gives us moments, and for those moments we live.

Questions to Consider

Where is unbridled joy? Is it present in me here and now? If not, can I recall it? Is there an instance that brings it back to me? Where does it go when it is absent?

_____

_____

_____

_____

_____

_____

_____

THANKSGIVING

THANKSGIVING. The only major holiday that does not salute a particular religion or group of people or encourage alcohol consumption. It is blind to race, creed, or nationality. Commercialism is minimal other than for the food we purchase to gorge ourselves. Observed by most everyone, the only requirement is an acknowledgment of gratitude.

Frankly, it is surprising to me that no group has co-opted the Thanksgiving holiday. Imagine that. Not business or veterans, not patriots or Christians, not labor unions or the Irish. No one has laid claim to the day. Consequently, even atheists and anarchists can participate.

These thoughts came to me as I watched my daughter's middle school orchestra classes come together for a concert. It was an equal opportunity gathering without political or school administrator speeches, no teacher or child singled out. Kids and parents of every color and belief were there, a community activity with everyone sharing. So it is with Thanksgiving.

As I sat beaming, not just at Brianne and the music, but at this whole collection of pleased faces, I considered this notion of giving thanks. There is much more than meets the eye. I thought of a friend in Albany, New York where I once resided. Pete is a Christian Brother and has a profound perception of thankfulness. Indeed his motto for living is in his own words: "To maintain an attitude of gratitude." I must say, his life seems to demonstrate that an attitude of thanks can dispel all manner of resentments, unhappiness, and animosity.

I know many readers think such a notion to be hopelessly idealistic and naïve. Still, Pete's life proves that it is possible to strive for such an ideal and attain much, which would otherwise remain beyond our grasp. His is nothing more than the wisdom the masters have sought to teach us. Jesus said, "In everything give thanks". Eastern sages might say, "What is…is good." What a revolutionary concept. Can you imagine seeing everything thankfully? Through eyes freed of all negative expectations? Therein would seem to lie something extraordinary.

With these thoughts before you, allow me to share my prayer with you for Thanksgiving and each day to come:

"Thank you for all that I have and all that I lack as well. I'm grateful for the presence of friends and family, and all those absent due to distance and death. Thank you for pleasure and pain, joy and hardship. Grant me one simple wish, for all those for whom I harbor ill will, resentment, and envy, and for each who has wronged or frightened me whether neighbor, friend, or foe, bless them with the peace and contentment I wish for myself. Thank you for life."

Afterthoughts

I have learned that at my best, happiness and gratitude are a choice. Now that is not to say that we should practice positive thinking, what in olden scriptural days would have been called "whitewashing the sepulcher," placing a pretty coat of paint on something that stinks because it contains dead bodies. Rather, that on the other side of the ugly truth is peace.

The power of choice has always come to me with the admission of the truth.

Questions to Consider

What is there in my life for which to be grateful? Do I feel grateful? Can I choose gratitude? Without denying the truth?

TELL TALE AGING

WHEN you're young, you hear many stories of aging. These tales have no effect; they're irrelevant. Then one day, reality creeps into your life.

It happened to me as I opened a kitchen drawer in search of a plastic bag. There sat a bag of formerly frozen broccoli. The odor of rotting vegetables wafted upward.

A belly laugh ensued. I knew immediately what had happened. I had sought a twist tie to close the freshly opened bag, carefully sealed the bag, then promptly dropped it into the drawer.

Now I could pass this off as an isolated moment of distraction, but I would be practicing denial. The truth is that my forty-six year old memory is showing the initial signs of frailty due to aging. That matches an emerging pattern of lost words and vivid concepts that my brain simply can't articulate at times.

Now I could go toward either of two socially acceptable norms with the situation. I could bombard myself with efforts to deny aging its due: CoQ10, Ginko Biloba, memory building devices, and so forth. If I pursue this direction fully, I'll soon find myself drinking strange concoctions and working out feverishly at the gym, perhaps going so far as plastic surgery, hair implants, blonde babes, and a red sports car.

On the other hand, I could follow the crotchety route of complaining and whining. I would seek to meet societal expectations for an aging person beset with lamentations and woes.

At this point, I'm simply observing the process. My hair is graying and thinning. I am sagging. Toilet habits really are becoming quite important.

So what is to become of me? Well, regardless of any path I choose, I'm going to die. There's that uncomfortable truth. Aging is only the beginning of my demise.

My great hope is to learn to do this aging thing graciously and gracefully…to not whine…to become wise rather than shallow…to see the beauty of it all, rather than to resist at all costs.

If I am successful, I expect to be able to keep laughing at the absurdities of it all. At least, that is my hope and aim.

Afterthoughts

Once, two friends nicknamed me Earnest in recognition of an exceedingly serious perspective on life. And I'm still prone to taking matters pretty seriously. Fortunately that lifts on occasion, and I become able to embrace the less desirable aspects of life, and see, with humor.

Questions to Consider

Do I see humor in my life? When does it occur? Is it ever associated with difficulties? Why or why not?

_____

_____

_____

_____

_____

_____

_____

_____

RIGHT AND WRONG

IT was 1982 and I was twenty-six years old, a recent graduate of a highly regarded corporate financial training program and in charge of certain accounting operations at a manufacturing facility in Shreveport, Louisiana.

I was full of youthful exuberance, energy, and pride; I was a typical young man with a great amount of education and newly found authority, certainly cocky and probably arrogant. One day I had to make a decision on a man's pay. I followed the guidelines scrupulously and zealously, concluding we need not rectify an error in his pay until the next payroll. It was a correct interpretation of policy.

On payday I was summoned to meet with the man. He was tall and large, and wore a blue, sleeveless workshirt. I approached him, hand extended, and introduced myself. I asked him how I might help him, to which he responded that his pay had been short and he desired an advance. I launched into a lengthy, overly complex explanation. His eyes never left mine, though I periodically looked away in discomfort. I summoned all my authority and concluded by telling him our policy did not allow for small advances such as this and that we would correct it in next week's pay.

The man stepped a bit closer to me and peered down with a hint of a scowl upon his face. He studied me for a moment, sizing me up, I think. Then he spoke slowly and carefully. "Look, I don't know about all your rules and guidelines. But what I do know is there are a few things you don't know. Let me tell you how it is. You don't mess with me, you don't mess with my woman, you don't mess with my truck, and… you sure as hell don't mess with my pay. Now, are you going to fix this or not?"

I was daunted and I could feel my injured pride. But while my position may have been right, I was wrong. In my condescending attitude, in my righteousness, even in the rules and guidelines, I failed to see beyond to what was right.

I corrected his pay on the spot. Quietly and courteously he thanked me and returned to his work.

I have never forgotten that experience. It was a short interaction, which taught me an immense amount. My education, my position, my rules, and my demeanor obscured what was right. In retrospect I gained some humility that day. For the first time I knew that actions might be wrong even though within the proper bounds. More importantly, he taught me to listen for perspectives other than my own and to know beyond any doubt, the other fellow may be right.

Afterthoughts

There is a phrase that is appropriate to my life; "Everything I let go of has claw marks on it." It seems that letting go of my certainties has probably been the hardest lesson of my life.

I remember a therapy session where a notion about relationships came into question. I almost leapt at the therapist, "Don't you understand? This is how it is!"

I think my certainties, my rights and wrongs, make me feel secure. Security is, after all, nothing more than perceiving the world around us to be consistent with our beliefs.

Questions to Consider

What would I be like if my beliefs about right and wrong simply vanished? How would I feel if my certainties were shown to be false? What if the world is not as I believe it to be?

_____

_____

_____

_____

_____

_____

_____

POCKET WATCHES

A number of years ago I got tired of beating up wristwatches, a frequent occurrence with me, and decided to switch to pocket watches. In the interim I have had no reason to question that decision, I love pocket watches.

In the first place, there is some incredibly cool aspect to them. Perhaps it is the telltale chain holding them to a belt-loop or vest. Maybe it's the large face. Or it could simply be the comforting act of removing the watch and the rhythm of the motions needed to check the time or wind it.

While it may not be convenient like a wristwatch, this is one of those cases when ease strikes me as the inferior attribute when compared to the beauty and elegance of a pocket watch.

For the longest time my watch was a rather non-descript affair with a gold cover. Then in 1990 I felt an urge that led to a series of local watchmakers. I executed my usual shopping pattern, poking around endlessly, certain that when I found the right one I would instinctively know it. The event came to pass in a small, out of the way shop. After surveying several restored antique watches, I asked the proprietor if he had any others. He shook his head, but then checked himself. "Well, there is one I've been working on," he muttered. He disappeared into his workshop for a few moments before returning with a small cloth bag. Laying out a felt display cloth, he carefully slid the pocket watch from its cover. It was a burnished, dark gold with a large porcelain face. I was smitten, and we negotiated a price for the continuation of its refurbishment.

When I picked it up two weeks later, I was delighted. So much so that my zeal got the better of me. That night I went rollerskating with it in my pocket. Of course I crashed, smashing the crystal and breaking a few inner mechanisms. I was crushed.

Fortunately it was reparable, though I felt quite the fool. I remembered childhood admonishments to never attach so much value to anything, lest it perish or fail. I saw I had been a bit too enthralled with the watch and made it a point to be a little less adoring when I picked it up from the watchmaker.

One of the pleasures of owning such a finely crafted work surfaces through the care it requires. I've sought out fine craftsmen, master watchmakers to keep it in operating condition. Frankly, I have always been slightly in awe of such a high level of skills as those in craftsmen. In a time of mass produced, disposable products, interaction with these meticulous and talented masters is pure pleasure. And I value my watch all the more.

The antique Burlington watch in my pocket is less reliable than the mechanical pieces found everywhere. It is also more expensive to maintain. And I mentioned it may be less convenient. But if all that matters is efficiency and cost effectiveness, there is little room for beauty and craft. This pocket watch is proof of a different and somehow finer type of quality, a gentle reminder of values beyond those of the marketplace of modern days.

Afterthoughts

I wince as I see I must admit a truth.

I am vain. About pocket watches. About my profession. About words and books. And especially, I am vain about being contrary in my perspectives.

Vanity is false perception, identifying with attributes, which in fact become veils.

I think my vanity must be my greatest impediment.

Questions to Consider

With what possessions or attributes am I identified? What do those false identities provide to me?

_____

_____

_____

_____

_____

_____

_____

KREBS, OKLAHOMA

MCALESTER, Oklahoma, my hometown, is a small city of some twenty thousand people located in the southeast corner of the state. Wooded with scrub oaks, it is interspersed with large hills and open pasture. It is average country, neither particularly hot nor cold, not plains nor mountains, fairly open and friendly folk of many races and mixed nationalities, and economically middle class.

Just down the road is the town of Krebs. How Krebs came to be is one of those generally unknown curiosities, which few would ever question. A very small town comprised of numerous Italian families, their forefathers came as manual laborers seeking opportunity through now defunct coal mines. Krebs, though a tiny community, had three outstanding Italian restaurants when I was a kid: Pete's Place, Minnie's, and Isle of Capri. Just a few miles away on the highway bypass was Dom Giacomo's Place.

I remember family visits to Pete's Place where we would be seated together in a separate room of the old house. All menu items were accompanied by heaping family style platters of tossed salad, fresh garlic bread, and spaghetti in meat sauce. Refills were upon request. And there was ravioli…monstrous, meat-filled ravioli. In a word, extraordinary. For a growing boy it was nirvana. For my parents trying to keep a family of six well fed, it was a great deal.

Last year, while visiting my father en route to a vacation in Arkansas, my wife, daughter, and nephew went with Dad and me, to Pete's. They have expanded, renovated, and tastefully redecorated. The platters don't seem as large and laden as once they appeared, though it could be no more than a boy's jaded and vivid memories that are faulty. Nonetheless, time had not dulled the flavor of fine cooking. Lest you think me bedazzled by nostalgia, my family raved unanimously, four stars in our book, and my dad ate until I thought he might burst. They still talk in a dazed sort of way when recalling the ravioli.

My return to Krebs brought back memories beyond ravioli. Especially, I recalled Labor Day, when the town would swell with people viewing the terrapin races in the town center. My friends and I, mischievous and delinquent, would lob water balloons over city hall to splatter among the box turtles, driving them into their shells and exasperating fans and gamblers. Laughing uproariously, we avoided town officials intent on catching us. We would cruise by giant tanks holding fifty-pound catfish and three-foot long snapping turtles, muttering macho teen-aged dares to grab the turtles by their massive snouts. I would hope to see my first true love, Bernadette.

We would jump on our motorcycles and race to a friend's father's ranch where we would jump ravines, dodge cattle, splash mud, and pop wheelies. Then off we would fly to the old abandoned coal mines to spurt madly up and down huge slag piles as black dust coated our cycles and bodies.

I suppose like any memories, these must be suspect, even dangerously idyllic. But the return to Pete's Place proved that some pleasant recollections are not fantasy. The ravioli proved that.

When next you find yourself passing through southeastern Oklahoma on the Indian Nations Turnpike or US Highway 69, take a few minutes to visit Krebs, just east of McAlester. Stop at the town hall and imagine the area packed with raucous laughing residents watching eastern box turtles race. Look around. Take a few breaths. Go to Pete's Place. Order the ravioli. You will not be disappointed. My memories will be yours as well. Who knows, you may even recall teen-aged rapture and the magnificence of youthful madness.

Afterthoughts

I'm smiling as I remember. But that has been a long time in coming. For too long I, like many, was conflicted about my adolescent years, some of which were indeed quite mad. A lot of damage resulted.

Yet I can now say that I am at peace with it all. That's saying a lot, especially since I was troubled enough to practice some self-mutilation and seriously considered suicide on a number of occasions.

Peace is a great gift, the result of inner peacemaking, which may be the purpose of our lives.

Questions to Consider

Am I at peace with my life and my history? Where am I yet obstructed and pained? What would it take to set myself free?

_____

_____

_____

_____

_____

_____

_____

_____

THREE TALES

THERE were two men whose car had broken down and they had taken a shortcut across a pasture toward a distant farmhouse. Half way across the field they suddenly realized there was a massive bull with long, ugly horns closing the distance between them at a brisk pace. The men accelerated, as did the bull. Realizing they were in trouble, the men began to run but the bull was rapidly gaining.

One man turned to the other and gasped, "Quick! This is getting bad! You're religious, say a prayer to get us out of this!"

The second man wheezily responded, "I can't think of one! Too distracted!"

The first man snapped, "Say anything, anything at all! We're about to get killed!"

It was silent for a moment except for their labored breaths and the sound of thundering hooves. Then the second man bellowed, "Lord, for what we are about to receive, may we truly be thankful!"

****

I would like to share three inspiring tales from my life for which I hope you will "truly be thankful," of course without the motivation of a bull.

It has been my experience that the inspirational and insightful moments of each of our lives are like manna from heaven, and they are meant to be shared with others. In doing so, we both may benefit.

When I married for the second time, Regina came as a package deal with two daughters. And I came horribly prepared to be a parent, both in demeanor and skills. I was instantly swept away by demands that were beyond me. I stumbled. I fumbled. I screwed up badly. Emotionally, I was in over my head. I experienced despair as a result of my failings. It really did seem hopeless.

Over five discouraging years I worked with counselors as well as my life mentor. It was an ugly and painful process. More than a few times I wanted to flee. It seemed much easier to accept failure than to continue to confront it.

One day, which was utterly ordinary by all accounts, I was talking to Sam, my life mentor. We were rehashing my latest failings when he suddenly hushed me. Then he said in his slow, Texas drawl, "Ron, you are doing your best, and that has to be good enough." For some inexplicable reason it struck me full force.

Sam told me to write it down as part of my morning prayers. "Thank you God that my best is good enough." Several years later I continue to write the words daily and now I offer them to you. No matter your circumstances, "You are doing your best, and that has to be good enough."

During another trying episode in my life, I was dismissed from my position with a company in which I had invested over ten years. I'd heard it said that, "If you've never been fired from a job, you've not pushed the limits sufficiently." When I was let go, I did not feel very inspired by that supposed wisdom.

Fortunately I received excellent placement and career guidance. I returned to school for a graduate degree in Social Welfare and specialized in organizational development and change. It was a gift, an extraordinary blessing. And along the way I came by a second item that is written into my morning prayers on a daily basis. "Thank you God that my happiness is not dependent on anything or anyone." I had learned, as I hope you may as well, that job or no job, spouse or no spouse, money or not, my happiness is not conditional.

My third daily written prayer actually comes from a management workshop in which I participated when I was only twenty-three years old. The leader's task was to teach us to be leaders, and much of the material revolved around effective management techniques.

On the last day of the weeklong training, he astounded me when he shifted gears as part of his leadership presentation. He said in a strident voice, "You are here because of who you are. If anyone, anywhere, including this corporation, ever asks you to be or to do anything that is inconsistent with who you are, pack your bags and your briefcase. Go. And don't look back. If you sacrifice who you are, that which brought you to be here, you are undermining all that you represent and all that matters."

And from that comes my third prayer of affirmation. "God, thank you for making me as I am."

I do not know your life. I cannot know your life anymore than you can know mine. But I can tell you of the experiences which have transformed and bettered me. These three comprise a large part of the prayer, which is my life.

Thank you God that my best is good enough.

Thank you that my happiness is not dependent on anything or anyone.

God. Thank you for making me as I am.

As each of you proceed through this day, this experience, and this life, I hope my experiences may be useful to you. I hope your life is or becomes a glorious and beautiful prayer. And I hope that each of you remembers to share your experience, strength and hope with others. In the end, nothing else matters.

Afterthoughts

On another speaking occasion, I wanted to share the hope that fuels so much of my life. Despite despair, seeming failure, and no small amount of confusion, somewhere within me is a well of hope that always abounds.

If, in fact, God is compassionate, omnipresent, and all knowing, then it is only my limited perspective that is lacking.

Questions to Consider

Do I believe my best to be sufficient? Is my well being dependent on anyone or anything? Do I appreciate myself?

IN RELATIONSHIP

UNUSUAL FORTUNE

"CANCER." An awkward pause followed. Sam repeated himself, "Cancer." Then he added, "The tests indicate prostate cancer."

I have known Sam since 1990. To say he is a friend is a vast understatement. I refer to him as my mentor, for no other word adequately describes one who counsels, encourages, guides and listens. He assisted me with marriage, the death of my mother, several traumatic career changes, my prayer life...all those important matters of life.

It was not surprising that his announcement stunned me. I feared losing him. After a quiet, but prolonged moment, I managed to escape my self-absorption and asked him how he felt.

His response is indelibly imprinted in my memory. He raised his eyebrows slightly and shrugged with a shake of his head. He looked me straight in the eye as the corners of his mouth canted upward in a hint of a smile.

"Ron," he said, "This is going to be quite a learning opportunity."

His was a matter-of-fact statement, but suggesting curiosity. Later, I found myself contemplating his response. Actually, I was awestruck. Imagine, I thought, a diagnosis of cancer causing nothing more than an intense interest, not even a suggestion of fear.

At first, I convinced myself he was using the power of positive thinking, that sometimes annoying life philosophy which insists on finding virtue in death, illness and misfortune. Arlo Guthrie once summarized it well, "You can't have a light without a dark to stick it in." Funny guy. His was just an improved version of the questionable childhood wisdom of how we would never appreciate the good were it not for the bad.

As Sam and I spoke over ensuing weeks, I observed he was not practicing positive thinking. There was something authentic about his openness to his illness. I began to see that Sam actually embraced this apparently awful diagnosis. Moreover, he was genuinely grateful, trusting the current of life and the cancer as a part of life.

I contrasted that with the resistance of my own life. I was suddenly weary of my burdens as well as envious of Sam's grace. I made a vow that someday I would come to embrace whatever may come to me, not to become an optimist, rather to engage the events of my life with relish and pleasure.

nething miraculous occurred. Not to me, but Sam's cancer diagnosis turned

'ests were wrong, or perhaps something extraordinary did occur. Regardless,

much of the rigidity and fear, which formerly bound me, has diminished

ems I have not been quite the same since that inspired moment when I

ife. Sam's experience and actions taught me, though words seem woefully

what I have learned.

myself experiencing a deep and abiding sense of gratitude. "In everything give thanks,"

cal prophet. Strangely, that notion is no longer so far fetched. Even in the midst of discomfort,

pain, I do not resist as much as once I did. I feel comforted quite often. I am not always happy, but

I have never been so contented.

I remember the tingle which ran up my spine in 1977 when I first saw the movie "Star Wars." Do you remember Obi Wan Kenobi's words to Luke Skywalker, just before he attacked and destroyed the Death Star? "Luke! Trust the force!"

I have not yet learned to fully trust, to freely cast myself into the torrent of life with abandon. Nevertheless, I no longer battle so fervently. It seems I am being changed.

I am a lucky man. I am en route to a full and grateful heart.

Afterthoughts

Another mentor, Patrick, who preceded Sam in my life, once told me that as we tend to the affairs of the heart and soul, changes would come. Yet the changes would appear mysteriously, and if asked what I had done or when it had come to pass, I would not know.

Life is shaping me at every moment. Like the river that overnight changes its course, the moment of change is preceded by ten thousand days and the inexorable shifting of a trillion grains of sand.

Questions to Consider

From whom have I learned? Was I taught by their words or actions? Do I see the role they played at that time?

_____

_____

_____

_____

_____

_____

_____

_____

A MYTH REVEALED

MY tale begins in 1985 in the midst of a significant opportunity, during which time my first wife abandoned me. The ensuing difficulties overcame me. Three years later in 1988, because of all the changes and my inability to cope with them, I was released by the corporation that I had aspired to lead. I thought myself broken.

It was then that I began to learn that self-made men and women are a myth, despite the stories we hear of people pulling themselves up from poverty or hardship. It was my good fortune to be placed into "outplacement" by the corporation, which protected my income for a time and provided me with career counseling and other supportive services. The counselor who assisted me taught me a great deal, but her most brilliant stroke was to assign me the task of interviewing at least five elderly men or women whom I respected. My goal was to understand the course of their lives and careers.

To my surprise, not one of those with whom I spoke, nor dozens of others whose stories I later sought, could have predicted the course of their lives. One man wanted only to be a surfer and beach bum, but was required by the state of California to regularly interview for jobs in order to collect unemployment. He interviewed for an accounting job with a major defense contractor in a tank top and swimsuit; he was on his way to the beach. That company saw something in him and offered a position, which led many years later to his promotion to division controller.

In Albany, New York I met a woman who had a strange experience. She was driving through that fair city in 1970 on the New York State Thruway. During a stop for a cup of coffee, she fell in love. She lived in that city for the rest of her life.

My favorite life story comes from Jim Peterson, a seventy-eight year old man living in Albuquerque, New Mexico, who survived the beaches of Normandy on D-Day because, in his own words, "I got drunk and passed out in a ditch. Came to, surrounded by dead Germans. I will never forget the look on the face of the military policeman who saw me crawling out of that ditch, back from the dead. Getting drunk saved my life."

What I have learned from my elders is that our lives are not our own. I believe it is grace, but you may call it what you wish: fate, circumstance, or good fortune. The facts remain that it is parents and other adults who teach us how to live our lives, genetics which fosters much for which we claim credit, patriots who created a country where we could be free to thrive, as well as doctors, researchers and inventors whose work allows us to live a comfortable, healthy and long life. These are the authors of our lives!

My own life is proof; I have arisen like a phoenix from the ashes of my own personal hell. I now have a new life, a different career, a beautiful second wife and two daughters. By all appearances, I am a self-made and successful man. Yet, how can I claim credit? It was family and friends who nurtured and supported me in a time of great personal trauma. Furthermore, a number of clergy, therapists, physicians, and educators put my life back together.

Despite the voice in my head that insists I can take credit for my marvelous successes, the truth remains that I am beholden to untold numbers of people and circumstances of which I am utterly ignorant. This is true even of my first wife's departure and my dismissal from my former employer. Without their actions, I could not be here now. Indeed, I am overwhelmingly indebted.

Because of my experiences, I know there are no self-made men and women. That is a myth. We are the products of grace and happenstance beyond our understanding. How fortunate we are. That is reason enough to graciously and generously share our lives and everything we have received so freely.

Afterthoughts

I've just returned from a long hike. I meditated in the hot sun while a breeze played across my face. For those few moments my mind quieted and I felt a peace descend upon me.

I can feel the presence of God. It is palpable. It is omnipresent. It simply is. And it is totally unearned. Nothing I have done has caused its visitation. I can claim nothing.

Questions to Consider

What do I usually claim credit for in my life? Can I find evidence that attributes it to me? Can I see the activities of others in it?

_____

_____

_____

_____

_____

_____

_____

CARROTS FOR BUSTER

IT was a delightful spring merging into a brilliant but yet mild summer. After several years spent carefully learning from the challenges and tribulations of gardening, my wife and I had concocted a superb plan that resulted in a glorious garden. This year we would be free of scourges and blights.

Garlic and marigolds surrounded tomatoes and carrots. Zucchini vines shot up a trellis to foil the incursion of squash bugs. Spinach languished under the shelter of the apricot tree. Aromatic tobacco dust encircled stalks prone to borers and caterpillars. The elegance of the design and beauty of the plantings delighted us.

Far greater writers than I have spoken of the marvels of gardening and the virtues of working the earth with dirtied hand. And far greater gardeners have wrested bounty from tilled soil. But that cannot diminish the satisfaction to those of us of lesser skill.

So it came as some surprise when we discovered that we had one significant omission in our planning. We failed to account for the potential for brilliance from our beloved Chinese Pug, Buster.

Now the dog book we own states that Pugs are sadly lacking in utility. Bred to sit on the laps of emperors and empresses, they have no valuable or even meaningful function. Their clownish appearances suggest limited intellect. But there is no underestimating the aptitude of a dog whose will is principally governed by the pursuit of his next meal.

It was early evening when I looked out the patio door. Buster stood stalk still except for the twitching of his muzzle beneath which dangled a beard of carrot greens slowly swaying in the breeze.

Carrots…Buster's favorite snack treat. But how did he discover them?

We remembered that we had unearthed one on the previous day and fed it to him. He made the connection. Buster moved from a ward of the household to grazing, a giant leap no doubt. And one not considered by our best-laid plans.

A crafty, foraging dog. Next year, we will add a fence to the garden.

Afterthoughts

Relationships with dogs form a foundation in my life. As long as I can recall, I have felt safe and secure with animals, and especially close to dogs. I don't know why, but I adore them.

Questions to Consider

What is the nature of relating in my life? Is it defined by the other party or object, by the connection with them, or does it reside within me?

_____

_____

_____

_____

_____

_____

_____

_____

GOOD IS THE ENEMY OF BEST

I am one of those people who is always repeating some little saying to myself in order to live a little more of the life to which I aspire. In Eastern thought, they call these sayings "mantras." I regularly write them in my daily planner as reminders. Still, they fade away as they lose their power to motivate or inspire, though a few recur over the years.

For example, the phrase "pay attention" has come to me often, each time in moments of profound awareness of mystery, natural beauty, and grace. But inevitably the mantra ceases to provoke my attention and slips once more into the murky depths of my mind, until events again conspire to push it forth.

Recently I experienced one of my favorite mantras as I floated amid nostalgic memories of a past romance. Sheila was a fine woman: sensitive, thoughtful, and attentive. She and I were involved for nine months in a very good relationship. Yet I could not free myself from a disconcerted feeling that it was not what I totally desired. I agonized for what seemed like an eternity, but in reality was only four weeks. One day as I chatted with a wise friend over coffee, I related my difficulties. In characteristic fashion, Patrick refrained from giving advice, then gently offered me a pearl of wisdom: "Ron, never forget that good is the enemy of best. All you need do is ask yourself, 'Is this good, or is this best?' Intuitively you will know."

He was right, in a few days I knew I must end the relationship with Sheila. Another few days passed before I could overcome my fear of releasing the known, that which was good. After all, it is so easy to settle.

I managed to do it, though I could not find words to express my situation. How do you tell a loved one they are not "best?"

Within a few months I had decided to move to Albuquerque, a lifelong dream. Eighteen months later I was married here in a church in the Valley, to Regina. All this came to pass as a consequence of a simple saying. I cannot tell you the number of times the "good or best" mantra has resurfaced in my life. Certainly it has appeared frequently on the pages of my planner and guided many of my decisions.

These thoughts emerged this week as Regina related the story of her courageous decision to divorce her first husband. But this time she included her former mother-in-law's words as she attempted to dissuade Regina from divorce. "Hon, the world and our lives are not perfect. We have to settle for what we have."

Regina sought more than settling. She tried for the best, and she thinks she found it. Based on my experience, there is one message I ought to carry forth to everyone I meet. The good is the enemy of the best. Don't settle. Life is too precious to have less than our heart's desire.

Afterthoughts

It is said that God will constantly reveal more to us. That is certainly my experience.
I have never been more content than now, yet I seem to always be in pursuit of something more.
Perhaps that which is "best" is always evolving.

Questions to Consider

What's best for me? Have I settled? Why or why not?

_____

_____

_____

_____

_____

_____

_____

LOVING YOUR WIFE

ACCORDING to a friend who is a florist, most of us do very little in the way of recognizing others except for significant occasions. She seems to think nothing of it and considers such behavior to be normal. It is unfortunate that such complacency has become commonplace. I have learned much about this subject because I am very self-centered. In fact my first marriage ended because of my selfishness.

Eleven years ago my first wife, Melanie, rolled over in bed and told me she no longer loved me and intended to leave the marriage. Her words stunned me. The moment felt surreal, almost fictional. Worse still, I felt terribly foolish for I thought all was well. Obviously, I was deluded.

There was little to be done. The relationship had died a slow death over seven years. While it was not the sole problem in our relationship, the neglect I ignorantly imposed upon this woman was a significant factor. To be more precise, I paid too much attention to jobs, chores, and golf. In the end, a love, which was once ripe and lush, wilted like a plant deprived of life sustaining water. Painfully, I learned that relationships must be tended and nurtured. They require an investment of effort. While I learned this too late to salvage that first marriage, I made a vow I would never again fail in relationships as a result of neglect.

For the past six years I have been married to a most wonderful woman. It is not easy for me; a lifetime of selfishness is not readily changed. For that matter, it is difficult for Regina; living with a self-centered person can be quite exasperating. Regina knows I try, however, because I extend myself with small tokens of my love: notes, flowers, and the like. Though none are substantial, they are steady. These small gifts are most important as reminders to me to pay attention to Regina. I do this because it feels good. as well as to avoid the devastatingly painful consequences of neglect. Both are selfish intentions. Fortunately, Regina benefits from these selfish acts.

These thoughts and words came to me recently while I was at work. A woman who sits beside me received flowers from a co-worker as a gesture of thanks and acknowledgment. Her appreciation was so great, tears welled up in her eyes. All day long I watched a steady stream of people visit her and admire her flowers. She invited most of them. Her delight was a joy to observe.

During the course of the day, I overheard her speaking in a low voice to a friend. She was troubled that an acquaintance could be so generous while her husband rarely acknowledged her. We are often too distracted and self-focused to attend to our loved ones.

Two days earlier, I had encountered a friend at the florist's shop. I was taking Regina two stalks of glorious, red gladiolas, one of her favorites. My friend asked me about the occasion. I was embarrassed and stammered, "Nothing really, just a few flowers for Regina."

"Oh!" she said. "You're just loving your wife."

I felt my face brighten. She understood perfectly. I smiled and nodded, then slipped away. Her words have stayed with me for many months. I am pleased to have such a simple phrase to explain so much.

"Just loving my wife." Enough said.

Afterthoughts

    In recent years I have come to see that the mistake I so often make in relationships, both male and female, is to reify them. I take that which is fluid, alive and ever changing, and build a construct of it, freezing it into a fixed and known but life-defying thing. I take a verb – relate, and make of it a noun – relationship. In the process, that which I desire is slowly strangled under the weight of knowingness.

Questions to Consider

    In my intimate relationships, whether friend or lover, how much have I come to know of them? Do I see them with fresh vision, or the dead eyes of the past? Am I relating to them in the present, or as an illusion frozen in some long ago time?

_____
_____
_____
_____
_____
_____
_____
_____

BEYOND DOGMA

ONE bright, cool day I hiked into the high desert west of Albuquerque with my dogs Buster and Skidder. They are Pugs, compact sausages with black faces and flattened snouts. They are the latest in a succession of short, squat dogs I have known from my youth until now. I never knew their significance until that hike.

It was a fine day for an adventure. We covered a few miles into the heart of the area known as the West Mesa, quite a distance for my cobby companions. I sat upon a low ridge of earth to rest and to eat a small snack, crackers and raisins for me, hard dog biscuits for Buster and Skidder. I leaned back to gaze at the sky. It was very still and the brilliance of the sun caused me to close my eyes.

I do not know if I fell asleep or if what followed was a waking dream. But I thought I lifted myself from the soil, then sat bolt upright in shock. Buster sat before me in lotus position, rear legs crossed in the sand, belly soft and distended, upper legs relaxed and dangling loosely before him, eyes half lidded and cast downward. An aura of light surrounded him as he softly chanted words I could not make out.

He reminded me of Yoda, from "Star Wars," only plumper and softer. I stifled a laugh at the thought, but then paused. Yoda was a Jedi Master, perhaps Buster was more than he seemed. Just as that notion evaporated, Buster leveled his eyes at me. His gaze was steady and calm. I thought I heard him speak. His mouth and jowls were motionless but I clearly heard words.

"Listen!" he said.

Needless to say, Buster had my undivided attention.

The dog continued. "I have been with you before as Nee Nee, the beloved dog of your youth. When that life was abruptly ended by a car, I came to you once more as Fozzy, your dear companion for seven years until you had to give him away. Thereafter, I passed quickly and returned to you again in this body."

I must have looked quite amazed at this point, for Buster seemed to acknowledge my stare with a nod before resuming.

"Once, many lives ago, I swore allegiance to you. You were an evil, vile man, a nomad wandering the desert sands. You were a thief and a coward, a man who murdered sleeping men and women for their meager belongings. But within you lay a single spark of decency. I was the mangy cur you would sometimes gently feed, though more often you would kick me in your bitterness."

"When inevitably, your throat was slit by another of your ilk, whom you had cheated, and you lay in a pool of your own life's blood, you may recall that as the last ember of life died in your eyes, I stood and watched you in compassion. In that moment, for inexplicable reasons, but in recognition of that trace of decency within you, I chose to watch over you and guide you for as long as it would take for you to be capable of a worthy life."

"I have been with you in many lives since that time and have joyfully fulfilled my commitment. You need me no longer. Now, it is I who must leave you."

As I sat with mouth agape, Buster blessed me with a motion of his paw and laughed what I gather was a good, proper dog's laugh. Then, he spoke once more ever so quietly.

"It is a good life. Pay attention!"

He gazed at me for a moment through deep, patient eyes. In the next moment he simply vanished. Suddenly, I was certain I was awake. I quickly glanced around me. There sat Buster in a normal dog's posture studying me impassively. To his left, Skidder lay in the sand slowly glancing side to side between us. I shook my head as if to clear cobwebs from my thinking. Buster's gaze never wavered. I clucked my tongue and both pugs came to my side.

We sat for a long time in the afternoon sun. To this day, I have no explanation for my experience. Skidder has passed away, but when I watch Buster napping in the sun, or when I sit quietly beside Skidder's grave, I am no longer certain of what I know. But every now and again, I observe Buster watching me with knowing eyes. Always, I pause and acknowledge him with a reverent nod of my head.

Afterthoughts

As I write these words, my heart quickens to Buster who died only a few weeks ago. Not sadness, but hope, swells within me. I have nothing but my heart to tell me that there is a truth of some sort in the preceding tale. Certainly, Spirit cannot die, and certainly, Buster was animated by Spirit. Our paths will cross again.

Questions to Consider

What matters do I know to be true that violate what I've been told and taught? How can I know these things? What is the source of such knowing?

_____
_____
_____
_____
_____
_____
_____
_____

GREAT VALUE IN SMALL TALK

I listened to a friend, Peter, deliver an impromptu speech about learning to overcome social awkwardness, a dilemma with which I am acquainted. At one point, Peter used a phrase that lit up my mind and caused me to smile. Peter said that for many years he did not understand the great value in small talk. Immediately I conjured an image of a couple of old men sitting over a cracker barrel talking about the weather, which has not changed appreciably in a lifetime, and retelling old stories just one more time. Passing time in a relaxed ease, with no one to impress, no point to be made and no debate to be won.

I suspect the vivid mental picture is in direct response to a world gone crazy with urgency. Everywhere I turn my attention, I find strident voices, messages, and people. Newscasts and newspapers are fraught with drama. Talk shows and sitcoms seek topics that will grab the most attention. Advertising becomes louder and more garish. Buzz words rattle within me: overnight, drastic, guaranteed, value. The din of the world is rising to a manic pitch, carnival barkers all.

I find myself becoming reclusive. Especially, I have seen my visits to retail stores dwindling. In their efforts to seize my attention with loud music, boisterous employees, neon, glass, and mirrors, they have driven me away. So too have I retreated from television, most magazines, and a great amount of cinema.

I must sound old and decrepit: a primitive, a Neanderthal. But honestly, must everything be a big deal? Is there no longer space for small talk? I know when my attitude first began to shift. Ten years ago a friend urged me to turn off the radio in my car as an experiment. After recovering from the initial shock, I was amazed at the world and its events around me. It seems that by eliminating a small amount of the barrage of distractions, I became calmer, more attentive, and more selective.

Now over the ensuing years, it has become obvious to me that I have slowly weaned myself from the excitement, the adrenaline, the mania. I honestly believe the noise level is rising. And, I know beyond the slightest doubt, that my sensitivity has been heightened. This is bad news for anyone trying to get my attention. I am no longer interested in strident messages or messengers. In fact, I find most of them clownish and their words outlandish.

I aspire to quiet walks, and silent contemplation on my back porch. Even my speech is becoming less urgent, more like the geezers of my mental imagery. Watch more. Talk less. Laugh at the excess. Refuse to be incited.

Life is good. It always has been and probably always will be. Only after disengaging from all the excitement have I found such contentment. Great value in small talk. Peter is right. I have probably said too much already.

Afterthoughts

Just this morning, in line with work in an organization, I found myself exhorting the committee with whom I was consulting. Now, as I read these words, I realize I was caught in drama.

There is a saying I've heard a number of times. *"Don't sweat the small stuff...it's all small stuff."*

I've heard it said that adrenaline is as addictive as heroin. And, I know that excitement results in the secretion of adrenaline.

Perhaps giving up drama may not be so simple.

Questions to Consider

What produces excitement in my life? Do I like the excitement? Why or why not?

_____

_____

_____

_____

_____

_____

_____

_____

THE PURSUIT OF BEAUTY

I had one of those epiphanies just a few days ago. My wife, Regina, and I were walking out through the garage door to run an errand and I had turned to say goodbye to my thirteen-year-old daughter Brianne. At first I thought it was the oddly angled sunlight on her face. But then I studied her more closely. At either end of her eyebrows was the dark shadow of hair growing back. Puzzled I said, "Are you plucking your eyebrows?" Before I could utter another word my wife swept me away in a flurry of motion and jabber. At a safe distance she explained that my guess was accurate. My daughter had gotten carried away with plucking and her eyebrows were now returning.

I chuckled as I listened to my wife's explanation of my daughter's attempts to grow up and her horrible embarrassment over this particular episode. Then we spoke a little longer and I heard that virtually all women plucked unwanted hair routinely. Taught by mothers, grandmothers, peers, and teen magazines, it is a sign of coming-of-age.

A scowl replaced my grin. My beautiful and someday to be gorgeous daughter was being offered beginning instruction in the fine art of socially acceptable mutilation. Soon, she would worry about the shape of her body, perms to remake her hair, paints, glosses, cover-ups, and shadows to alter her appearance, and perfumes to make her smell sweet. Somewhere in this process she would decide how much bosom, midriff, or thigh to show, to be pleasing to men. Should she become extreme she might even choose to puncture her body for ornamentation, learn to vomit to stay slim, or permanently alter her body through surgery to make it conform to socially desirable standards.

What a terrible tragedy. This little girl is already beautiful and shows signs of growing into a stunningly attractive young woman. Yet she is being taught that she is not enough, that she must be altered and enhanced to be pretty. How can we espouse such rubbish at the same time we profess to be concerned about the well being and esteem of women?

Some will laugh at my naïveté. I have been told before that it's just part of having some fun with your body and appearance. Perhaps there are some women for whom that is true. But for many, I have sensed a painful and powerful lack beneath their pursuit of prettiness. For an adolescent, whether boy or girl, this is the proverbial fall from grace. A contented child is taught to be a defective adult. We should be ashamed as a society for perpetrating this denigrating practice on unsuspecting, gullible young women.

There is little more I can do. My beautiful daughter has embarked on an endless pursuit of a shallow social value. I am naïve, and that is the way of the world. Still, it is not right.

Afterthoughts

Once again I see how quickly I forget that every path is sacred, and that all life is a process. Brianne's pursuit of beauty is as much a part of life as is the loveliness of a morning glory.

It is so easy to fall asleep to the truth that either God is everything or God is nothing. Judgments arise so rapidly and mindlessly.

One teacher, Judy, has said it so clearly. "The only path is to adore it all."

Questions to Consider

What situation last provoked me from inner peace? Was I conscious of the provocation? Did I choose it? If not, how did it come to pass?

_____

_____

_____

_____

_____

_____

_____

_____

FATHER'S DAY

IT was Father's Day, 1995, yet another opportunity to be cynical. I've never been able to convince myself that Mother's and Father's Days are anything more than a marketing scheme to create retail sales. Not that parents aren't due some recognition. I would have to be utterly blind to think such a thing. Parents invest huge amounts of energy and time, to say nothing of money and tears in their offspring. But it seems demeaning to set aside an obligatory day of recognition.

Nonetheless, this Father's Day I am more aware than ever of my indebtedness to my father. He would not feel that I owe him anything and he would be surprised at those things for which I am grateful. Yet those things still need acknowledgment. No card or gift will suffice.

My father is a putterer, forever fixing or improving things. This trait lives on in me. And it is a mighty tribute that it does. There is nothing more useful than the willingness to work on things that break or need improvement. It is a creative act, full of human desire and energy. I love it, and I learned it by watching my father for years.

Remarkably, it is through this act of puttering that I learned to whistle. You see, my father whistles while he works, always in tune though musically ignorant. I remember him cogitating (that's his word) over a car that wouldn't start, looking, poking, thinking, and whistling all the while. And I'm just like him, I whistle too.

Over all those years, through some strange process, I learned to be responsible. I don't know what he did exactly, but today I receive extraordinary benefits for that gift, as do my family, friends, and acquaintances. Responsibility is a precious, and seemingly rare, commodity, a gift that keeps on giving.

I suspect I think like him too, logical and reasonable. This trait has stood me in good stead. The world has been willing to pay me handsomely for my thinking. I guess it's like passing on a trade, a livelihood. But somehow it is more than that.

Increasingly people tell me that I am a lot like my dad. The traits I've mentioned are certainly a part of that, as are my voice, wrinkled brow, and balding crown. There was a time when I would have been offended by the notion. You probably know the words, something like, "Not me, I'm not going to be like him."

But I'm a little older now, and hopefully a little wiser. I'm more inclined to say "Yeah, how about that." Someday, when I feel less inclined to justify myself, I'll probably just say "Thank you."

Happy Father's Day, Dad.

Afterthoughts

   When did I come to make peace with my Dad? I am profoundly aware that long-held resentments are no more. I have forgiven. Wounds, real and imagined, have healed. I love my Dad. Once, I would have been unable to consider, much less utter, such a thought.

Questions to Consider

   Can I see my parent's contributions to my life? Do I cling to ideas that they failed me? Are my parents as I thought?

_____

_____

_____

_____

_____

_____

_____

_____

SKIDDER

ONE of our dogs died over Easter weekend. Skidder was a pug and only eight years old. Her liver failed and she died of the toxins built up in her little body. It was sudden, only five days from the obvious onset and her final, labored breath. I am in shock, as are my wife Regina, and daughters Natalie and Brianne.

I knew instinctively that I would tell this story. A number of years ago, at a friend's memorial service, I heard that the measure of a life is in the effects it produces in other lives. These are the tangible proofs of another's existence. We are all products of our relationships with others, including dogs. Thus our stories of them are their memorial.

So, let me tell you of our dog Skidder (sometimes Pooky, amongst other affectionate nicknames), and of what she brought to me.

When I married Regina she brought with her a ready-made family, two daughters, two cats, Skidder, and her puppy Buster who was born just before I met Regina. Skidder instantly became my intrepid companion as we explored the West Mesa. She climbed each of the mesa's five volcanoes many times and traipsed along numerous arroyos and trails. Her zeal never flagged.

Skidder was remarkably attentive. My most vivid memory of her is standing almost aquiver, ears piqued, head slightly cocked, nose twitching, and eyes shifting about in curiosity. She was very good at paying attention. Perhaps it was this attentiveness that caused my wife to call Skidder my disciple, worshipping her pug god. Skidder adored me, and I her.

For Skidder there was much time for play, tenacious play. Her favorite game was pulling on old socks, knotted, to improve her grip with her teeth. We dubbed this game "Pug-of-war." She was a delight.

Perhaps Skidder's greatest gift to me was her demonstration of the art of basking. Through it she earned her nickname: the sun pug. She would sit erectly, facing the sun, tilt her head slightly back, close her eyes, and bask. Time would stand still for her then. Her quiet, meditative pose and demeanor will forever inspire me.

This past week, as her liver failed, these traits, which made her such a gift, slipped away. It pains me to consider her diminishment, for it was so unlike her. Yet all the while her attentiveness remained, for her eyes followed me everywhere.

This dog's short and vibrant life deeply enriched the lives of our family. I have never had a better companion than Skidder. She taught me of zeal and love for life. I can think of no greater memorial.

On Saturday morning she awoke for the last time after a quiet, but difficult night. She was no longer Skidder; her spirit was ebbing. But in the end she saw the sun rise once more, and sensed spring in the songs of the birds and fine odors of blossoming cherry trees.

Death has now come to our beloved Skidder and she rests beneath an apricot tree in our backyard. We will miss her.

Afterthoughts

It was the death of another Pug, Rue, that taught me how it is I come to love. Rue was terribly abused and had to be nursed back to health. It took some time for her to not flinch in my presence. The perpetrator was a male.

After several years, Rue came to be a delightful companion. But brain damage from her abuse ultimately threw her into seizures that proved to be fatal.

When Rue died I realized that the love I felt came from the investment I made of myself. I saw that those things into which I pour myself, I come to love. Loving always returns itself in full measure.

Questions to Consider

Who, or what, am I invested in? Why? Do I love them or it?

_____

_____

_____

_____

_____

_____

_____

MEMORIAL

A number of years ago I attended a funeral for a friend. Betsy's death was sudden and unexpected, leaving many people in a state of shock. After the service we were directed to a hall at the local civic theater for a memorial gathering. In this informal setting a friend of the family asked each person to consider how Betsy had affected them and what we would most remember about her. After a long and uncomfortable silence during which we reflected on Betsy's role in our lives, we were asked to share our thoughts with the group. He said, "The final proof of our lives is that which lives on in others. Each of us is a living memorial to Betsy, a tribute to her life. Each time we acknowledge her, she lives anew." The ensuing stories and conversation transformed a somber setting into a celebration of Betsy's life.

I often recall that day, not only as a tender and pleasant recollection of Betsy, but as a reminder. Each of us affects and is affected by others. Each of us lives in others as they live in us.

Occasionally I find myself in awe of these implications. This occurred recently when my sister-in-law came to visit with her husband and children. Their newborn son, Reginald Francis, is named after his grandfather, my wife's father. I never knew Reggie, he died on August 21, 1986 at the age of fifty-six, four years before I met his daughter.

Seeing his namesake triggered a crescendo of thoughts within me. Reggie bears an almost mystical reputation in the stories told of him. On more than a few occasions my wife has sensed his presence and seen its form. My daughter, Natalie, recalls awakening to his aura on a moonlit night seven years after his death. She says Grampy sought assurances his family was well. Reggie died from a cerebral virus. He passed away in a coma only after being told that his youngest daughter, my wife's sister, had arrived safely at a distant college. I am told he visibly relaxed, then was gone in a matter of hours.

Almost a year ago, I experienced similar thoughts about Reggie. We received a few of his belongings from my mother-in-law: a compilation of classic literature, a guitar, a violin, and a most beautiful watercolor of a vacant, rural highway in Northern New Mexico. If I am to believe the substance of the man, it could very well be that his spirit has touched me through his now bequeathed possessions.

Certainly, his legacy lives on. I hear it in the classical music which fills our home. Reggie adored Beethoven, Bach, and Mozart. My wife and youngest daughter, Brianne, are accomplished musicians as a result of his influence. The haunting strains of Pachelbel's "Canon in D" envelop me when they play the piano that belonged to my mother before she died. It's odd; I never really cared for classical music. Do you suppose the spirit of a man who died many years ago could be so large as to affect me, even now?

His most obvious memorial is my spouse, Regina, named after her father. I do not know, but I would probably recognize much in her had I known him. Regina says I am quite like him. Given our mutual love of cereal and ice cream, we would have probably grown quite fat in each other's company. I also share his love for red chile, that most distinctive New Mexican food. I laughed when I heard he preferred to eat his with saltines and dill pickle spears. I am a straight tortilla man. Regina tells me we would have probably played golf together. Sometimes she smiles when she says he would have liked me, especially because I am a good husband to her. Reggie loved his children dearly.

One day, I rode my bicycle through Old Town Albuquerque and passed the school named after him, Reginald F. Chavez Elementary School. Though he was the principal, it is still quite a memorial. I marveled at the impact he must have made, for public school systems are not known for such acts.

I have been told that everyone adored Reggie, his kindness and attentiveness. If the measure of a man is told by such legacies, Reggie's life was quite significant. In telling his story, his memorial grows greater still. Through acknowledgment of the impact of his life, he lives again, in me and in you, though we never knew him.

Afterthoughts

I remember a discussion with an acquaintance. I sought to explain my understanding that we are not "self-made," but constructions of countless influences including those of our culture, our ancestors, and our communities.

He would have none of that. We argued. I conceded, not because my notion was wrong, but because sometimes we simply cannot see such contributions.

Questions to Consider

Am I self made? If so, how do I explain the part played by genetics, cultural and political forefathers, or the environment I was born in into? If not, to whom is credit due?

DIVORCED

IT'S funny, I feel I can hear my mother's voice from beyond the grave asking, "What have you done now, Ron Jr.?" This comes in response to the quandary in my own mind as I face my second divorce, this one from Regina, my wife of almost ten years.

Again, her voice flutters in my mind. "You don't speak about things like this in public, Ron Jr."

Society seemingly agrees with the voice. The last time I spoke with substantial candor on the radio, Regina got two calls from friends telling her they couldn't believe I was so open about private matters.

But you see, I have nothing to hide and neither does Regina. Divorce is no longer a social stigma though for many it remains a sign of failure. And I suppose that's why I've decided to give voice to my thoughts. I'm not accustomed to failure anywhere in my personal or professional life. I am one of the more competent people I know, though obviously that competence may not extend to marriage.

Still, I remain troubled by the need to explain this divorce. Most everyone we know was quite surprised by the announcement. Immediately both of us were hit with a crescendo of comments and questions. "You seemed so happy together." "The perfect couple." "What went wrong?" "Where did you fail?"

How do you tell people that we didn't fail, when society's measure insists otherwise? How could one possibly explain the extraordinary efforts we both put forth to build a marriage built on honesty, trust and love? What picture could ever paint the maelstrom of feelings and unanswered questions that remain? Why can't people understand the possibility of an amicable, mutual, and gracious divorce?

The answer to all these difficult queries is beyond me. Actually, that's not quite true. The answer is that there is no answer. No explanation is necessary. None could possibly suffice.

Love and marriage are mysterious to me. Clearly, I come from a society that struggles with that mystery. I'm not sure we understand the first thing about love or marriage.

A dear, older friend said to me, "Be grateful for almost ten loving, wonderful years." I cling to that thought, rolling it around in my mind. Ten, mysterious, loving, wonderful years. That makes me a very fortunate man.

Afterthoughts

There are tears in my eyes and heartache as I read this piece. I was so upbeat when I wrote it. So certain, and yet questions linger. And sorrow.

I know time heals every wound and injury. But it never takes away my questions. I still wonder about the possibilities of saving my first marriage, ended almost twenty years ago.

Solace comes from the words of Sam, "What could have been was."

Questions to Consider

Do I yet harbor questions about seeming past failures? Why? To what end? What value do I yet hold on the past, the pain, the guilt, the shame, or the beliefs?

_____

_____

_____

_____

_____

_____

_____

_____

THE GORGE

TEN years ago, shortly after I moved to Albuquerque, I became friends with a man from Taos Pueblo. We worked together at a local non-profit organization. Donovan and I grew to appreciate each other. I was especially impressed with his sense of himself as well as the integrity he displayed throughout his life.

We parted ways after four years at the non-profit when I left to start my own business. Don and I stayed in touch. We each had an opportunity to be an employment reference for the other. Infrequent contact gave us a chance to keep a sense of the other's life. He worked his way into a superb job with one of the pueblos.

Recently, we arranged a visit at the pueblo. It was a bit awkward for both of us at first. However, after a few of the formalities of catching up we quickly rediscovered the pace and rhythm of conversation that I remember so fondly.

I was struck by how much we had changed in some ways. We had older children, increased lines on both our faces, and relationship challenges. These are the typical passage-of-life items.

Donovan took me into the Rio Grande Gorge to show me the confluence of the Rio Pueblo and Rio Grande. It was a special place for him, and I easily understood why. It was there that I discovered the timelessness of friendship. We hiked and chatted. Then we sat beside the rushing water throwing rocks. Soon we stood, hurling rocks at various targets. For two hours we jabbered. Nothing had really changed though the details were almost all different.

After going our separate ways, he to complete some paperwork, I to drive home to Albuquerque, I found myself crying as I drove. The heartfelt conversation shook some things loose. And I don't mean that in a bad way at all. I needed to shed those tears, and friendship was the catalyst that allowed them.

Donovan and I have agreed to visit the gorge again. We wanted to hike, throw more rocks, talk further, and body surf in what he calls the best spot in the world.

Someone once told me that for most of us the only opportunity we'll have to see God is as an expression through the eyes of another person. I like that idea, but more importantly, I like the experience. It doesn't happen frequently enough, but it's too good to miss.

Afterthoughts

Friends are such gifts, mysterious as they may be. Bruce Brown. Hal Lackey. Sharon Ott. Phil Auer. Paul Heller. Laurie Hoff. Peter Farris. Tom Levine. Each, and others unmentioned, is a part of an evergreen memorial within me.

Questions to Consider

What endures within me that holds such fondness? Is it no more than a chemical mechanism that retains the emotional and psychological? Or is there something greater to relating?

_____

_____

_____

_____

_____

_____

_____

_____

WHEN I WAS A CHILD…

"WHEN I was a child I spoke as a child…but when I became a man I gave up childish ways." -
I Corinthians, Chapter 13

****

That Biblical passage is part of a section that is probably used more often than any in marriage ceremonies. It is part of four paragraphs about love.

I learned a lesson on this subject when I was seventeen years old and competing in the Oklahoma state competition for original oration. This was 1973 with its civil unrest, Watergate, the Vietnam War, hippies, the drug culture and rock and roll. While all the other speakers were talking about huge social issues, in my naiveté I decided to preach about the need for love.

I bombed. But I had a good time with the speech while I was bombing.

I'm not going to repeat that particular mistake here. But I would like to share two experiences that have taught me all I need to know about love. And then to relate them to the biblical passage with which I began.

My first story took place in 1985. I was twenty-nine years old and had just received a significant promotion with the Fortune 100 corporation for whom I worked. I was highly successful with the potential to rise quite far in the corporation. My beautiful wife, Melanie, and I were en route to Albany, New York, our new home. One day of driving was left and we stopped in Hershey, Pennsylvania to visit her parents. That night, we went out for pizza and a few beers. When we arrived back at our hotel room, we made love. Then Melanie turned over in bed and said, "I don't love you anymore. I'm leaving."

I was devastated. Crushed. Something just didn't add up. I was experiencing the American Dream: college degree, beautiful wife, great job and career, excellent income, promising future, an already significant investment portfolio. How could this be?

The honest truth is the experience almost destroyed me. Everything I believed in came crashing down around me that day. And it took a good many years to reconstruct it. But it set me on a path to understand this love thing for myself. So out of crisis arose an opportunity.

Fast forward to 1997, twelve years later. I've completed a Master's Degree in Social Welfare. I have a new career as a self-employed consultant working with not-for-profit organizations. I had moved to Albuquerque, New Mexico a few years before, where I met my beloved second wife Regina, who came with two daughters, Natalie and Brianne, who are now my own children for all purposes.

I rebuilt my life one painstaking piece at a time and have continued to pursue my goal of learning to love and be loved. But Regina and I struggled despite therapy, prayer, self-help books and processes, and efforts to improve communication.

I approached the man who has become my life mentor. I did not want to fail at love again. I was willing to do anything. Sam told me, "Ron, love is a decision. It is action, not feeling." I stared at him dumbfounded, like a small child. I began to reply, "But, what about…" Sam cut me off with a gesture of his hand. "Ron, do you love her," he inquired. "Yes, but…" He cut me off again. "Love is a decision. Without condition. Either love her as she is, or move on." An awkward pause followed. I looked at Sam and stuttered, "Do you mean love her no matter what?" He smiled, nodded his head and said: "No matter what."

A few weeks later, after much soul searching, I told Regina I had made a decision to love her no matter what. Loving her was my choice and I intended to act upon my decision no matter how it might feel or seem.

Our relationship was transformed. I was transformed. I no longer had expectation of my beloved wife. She was free to be herself and I was much happier.

Fast forward, one more time to a few months ago. The divorce between Regina and I is final. It's painful to me. Despite all my best efforts, I have seemingly failed at love again.

But not really. I made a decision to love Regina no matter what. That decision has not been changed. Love is a decision. Action. Not feeling.

Regina and I are on the best of terms. We did not need a lawyer to settle our divorce. There is no animosity. I maintain relationships with both of my stepdaughters, in fact I continue to support them though they are not legally my responsibility.

Make no mistake, it hurts. I don't know that I understand it. But I have put aside childish things and finally become a man. Love is not a feeling. It is a decision. It is action. Even in divorce, seeming failure, love has triumphed. It just wasn't what I expected.

Afterthoughts

At the urging of a friend, I volunteered as a hospice worker for a time. My assignment was to expect nothing in return. Since hospice patients are dying, it's easier to expect nothing. They will not be alive for long, and most are focused on their passage, not on me.

I learned a great secret through that work. Without expectations it is easy, very easy, to love.

Questions to Consider

Do I love anyone without expectation? What would it take to do so?

_____

_____

_____

_____

_____

_____

_____

ORVILLE REDENBACHER IS DEAD

WHEN Orville Redenbacher, the king of popcorn, died, his passing touched me, for Redenbacher's product represents an important time in my life.

In the autumn of 1974, I left home to attend college, a rite of passage for many young men and women. I arrived at Valparaiso, Indiana to attend Valparaiso University, a small college located in the northwestern corner of that state.

Valparaiso lies in the middle of a vast Corn Belt, which sweeps westward from Ohio to Iowa. It is flat country and the butt of many jokes; but it is wholesome country as well, with staunch family values and the reliability of the farmers who inhabit much of it.

Just a few miles east of Valparaiso lays the small town of Wanatah, sitting amid thousands of acres of cornfields. Adjacent to the highway was the Chester Products Company, the producer of Redenbacher's finest hybrid popcorn. It was just about the time when Redenbacher was pursuing large-scale marketing and his product was as yet relatively unknown.

However, he was not unknown to the ravenous students of Valparaiso University. We were stereotypical students, perpetually broke and hungry. In addition to macaroni and cheese dinners, there was popcorn. Chester Products sold Redenbacher's corn in an inexpensive, five pound, generically labeled jug. I ate mountains of his popcorn.

Good Lord! Orville Redenbacher is dead! Memories bubble forth at the thought of the man. I do not know how it is that memories are stored in our minds such that the passing of a man I never knew, whose only link to me is popcorn, could generate such thoughts. Nevertheless, so it is.

I recall a bitterly cold night after the passage of a blizzard. My roommate and I returned from a visit with my family in Ohio; two female friends rode with us. It was just after midnight and absolutely black outside with only the faint light of distant stars. Our road hog, a classic, blue, Oldsmobile sedan nicknamed Betsy, chugged along. Suddenly, a shower of sparks flew from a front wheel. We pulled to the shoulder of the road two hours from Valparaiso. Amazingly enough, a passing car soon pulled over to assist us. A young man emerged. He told us to stay put while he ran into the nearby town of Peru to make a few calls for us. A van arrived shortly, driven by an off duty police officer. He was a friend of the man and had come to drive the two women on to the university, a four hour round trip. Another friend arrived driving a tow truck. We all departed, the police officer with our friends to Valparaiso, the wrecker with Betsy to a local mechanic, and my roommate and I to a farm belonging to the man's parents.

Upon arriving, he roused his father and told him our tale. The farmer nodded a number of times then sent his son on his way. He escorted us to a guest room. As he wished us a good night's rest, he told us we would be expected for breakfast at six, only a few hours away.

We awoke to a hearty, country breakfast. For a time, we drank coffee and chatted with the farmer and his wife. Afterwards, he drove us to town where the mechanic had already diagnosed the mechanical problems with the car. The farmer further aided us by escorting us to salvage yards and auto parts stores to acquire the necessary repair items. By early afternoon we were on the road once more.

This is the spirit of the country where Redenbacher's corn grew, where I returned many summers to attend corn boils when hundreds of ears of fresh, sweet corn would be purchased in massive burlap bags. The corn would be soaked in the husk overnight in ice water, then broiled over open flames. The husk would retain water, which would steam the corn to perfection as it roasted on the grill. We would tug the husk downward from the corn to form a handle to dip it in a vat of butter. The memory of salted butter and juice flowing over my chin is vivid more than twenty years later.

It was here that I found true love, only to be abandoned by her at her parents' behest. The pain of that loss still evokes a bittersweet sense, though it was doubtless for the best. Sometimes, I wonder what her life has become. Is she happy? Though the man I was then seems an utter stranger to me now, his experiences, joy, and tears have created me. Would she be a stranger to me as well?

I recall a zealous quest for the meaning of life. Though naive, I thought the search wondrous. I knew so very little, but thought I was invincible. The newness of my life was full and ripe within me.

In Redenbacher's country, I came of age and discarded much from my childhood. There were late night trips to Gary to the *El Corral* restaurant for burritos and jalapenos as well as mad, foolish trips to Lake Michigan at the peak of winter. Debates raged into the early morning hours, expanding the depths of my knowledge as well as defining the limits of my physical self. Experiences filled me, heart, mind and soul.

Eventually, I graduated and left Indiana. Still, I spent the next three years in the corn country of central Illinois, and then began a circuitous tour of the United States, which continues to this day.

I feel a fondness for a time and place, which no longer exists except within my memory. I never met Orville Redenbacher though I have heard he was kind and eccentric, with a deep and abiding passion for his popcorn. Nonetheless, he is a part of my life.

Thanks for the memories, Orville. God speed my friend.

Afterthoughts

Mystics have taught me that there is no separation, what is you is equally me. There is nothing of which I am not part.

Questions to Consider

What life events give meaning to me? How do they do so?

_____

_____

_____

_____

_____

_____

_____

_____

COURTSHIP

WELL, I never imagined myself writing this particular piece, not in a million years. But experience has a way of creeping up on you and teaching you things, willingly or unwillingly. So after substantial consideration and more than a little painful experience, I have become a convert to that old notion of courtship. I imagine elders chuckling at this very moment. I don't blame you. But for the benefit of those more youthful, here's my story. And I'm sticking to it.

I have now successfully completed two marriages. That was not the plan. And I'm a bit chagrined to admit it. For a guy who is accustomed to being fairly successful in his life, I would have never dreamed that I would have to admit that significant relationships baffle me.

Now I don't intend to batter myself. But I do need to point out what I've learned. In a nutshell, I've discovered there is a lot to be said for getting to know someone well before you sleep with them or make a significant commitment to them.

Surprisingly, the problem doesn't really lie with who that significant someone happens to be, nor what they believe, nor how they behave. The problem lies in who I think they are. When a guy like me, who is prone to going in over his head with reckless abandon, doesn't learn much about that significant someone, it sets up a troubling pattern. I find myself with unrealistic expectations. Then disappointment sets in, which leads to efforts to get them to be different, which inevitably leads to still greater difficulties.

It never occurred to me that the problem begins when I don't find out who they are before I go in over my head. And, I must admit it feels rather foolish for a bright guy like me to discover in his forties, that he's missed this rather significant point.

Nonetheless, it has shown me the value of courtship. If you don't sleep with them or commit to them prior to getting to know them, you just might come to important conclusions before you are, to quote one of my wise elders, "Committed beyond your original intent."

What a novel concept. Get to know them first. My only consolation is knowing that I'm not alone in this problem. Maybe my insight might be useful to others who have struggled in relationships, though probably not. It's just too much fun jumping into the deep end of the pool.

Afterthoughts

In my research into relating, I've discovered that I am prone to falling in love with an illusion in my mind. I see what I want to see, and feel what I want to feel. When I do so, I do not see my partner. But when I inevitably come to see them, I am disappointed they are not otherwise.

Questions to Consider

With whom am I in relationship? Do I see them, or are they simply a mirror of my wishes…an illusion? Do I complain about them? Should they be different, or should I alter my illusions?

_____

_____

_____

_____

_____

_____

_____

_____

TEARS

PLANTED in the recesses of my mind is a vivid recollection of the day my first wife, Melanie, left me. I remember sitting at the top of the staircase clutching my dogs to my chest and sobbing uncontrollably, beside myself with feelings of fear and grief. There were no words to express my hurt it seemed; all I could do was cry.

At that time, I had not wept for a very long time, not to any significant degree, since the day my beloved, boyhood dog was killed. *That* moment is also frozen in the depths of my memory for it was the day I ceased believing in God.

Nee Nee had been loose in the street when a car sped over the hill in front of our house. The impact snapped my dog's neck instantly. My father laid the corpse on a newspaper in the garage for burial the next morning.

I don't remember how I slept that night for I was devastated, but the next morning I arose to deliver my newspaper route. I knelt beside the small, white-haired body as tears cascaded over my cheeks. I prayed for God to return my dog to me because I knew God possessed the power of miracles.

If ever there was a fervent, faith-filled prayer it came from that little boy that day. Yet God did not restore my dog. In the end, I stifled my tears. I bitterly and unconsciously resolved to neither cry, nor believe, ever again. If this God could not, or would not, respond to such an urgent, honest request, that God could not be trusted no matter the testimonials of preachers and saints.

Two decades later, when I was abandoned by my wife, the pain was so wrenching that my resolution burst before its compelling force. Years of unvoiced and unknown loss poured forth unbidden. The explosion of emotion shook me. Fear of a seemingly unending rush of tears only added to the pain. I thought I would perish.

Another decade passed before I finally came to begin to comprehend my experience. At the time I knew a little girl named Kayla Ruth who was two years old. She had golden, curly hair and a big toothy grin with perfected dimples. Her mother would dress her in brilliant, tie-dyed sundresses that made Kayla radiant. She was beautiful.

Kayla Ruth was killed in a freak accident in 1995. At her memorial service I beheld terrible suffering. The grief I saw struck me a severe blow. One moment I had tears in my eyes, then it was as if I were profoundly awake and attentive. I felt detached from my surroundings, an observer.

A vision passed through my mind, an emotional portrait of a baby only moments after birth. That child was each of us as we left our mother's womb: warm, cushioned, buffered, and comfortable. Until our expulsion, our needs were perfectly met. Heaven on earth. Then we were thrust into a startling experience. We were afraid and disoriented. We didn't even know the language.

In response to our dilemma, we cried. And our tears were the expression of that which we could not express. An expression of the inexpressible.

With the passing of the vision, I realized that our tears have always been such as those. Whenever our feelings are so great that we lack words to express them, tears will spring to our eyes. An expression of the inexpressible.

I saw even more at the memorial service. As I watched Kayla's mother sobbing, I suddenly knew that tears are perfect prayer. No translation is required. They need not make sense, nor must they form meaningful communication. No explanation is needed. The full measure of our joy or sorrow is contained in them, and because of this, Spirit can respond perfectly. True communion lies within our tears. From this we are comforted.

Tears are perfect prayer. An expression of the inexpressible.

I thought of the example of the garden of Gethsemane where Jesus experienced the deepest of despair. We are told, "Jesus wept." And I understood a hopelessness so great that the master himself had no words for it and could not pray. So he cried.

Perfect prayer. No translation required.

Then a story come to me from the science fiction novel, *Dune* by Frank Hebert, which is set on a desert planet so arid that water is priceless. The messiah character in the novel weeps in grief over the murder of his father. The local people are awestruck for they have never seen water come from the eyes, their adaptation to the arid environment. A murmur is heard, "He gives water for the dead." Reverence permeates their reaction, a reverence held only for the most holy and sacred of acts.

I recalled the night before my mother's funeral as my father and I sat alone by the casket. Dad said, "Son, she was a wonderful woman." Then he burst into tears. I had never seen my father cry. Now, at Kayla Ruth's memorial, I understood words could not express his loss and pain.

When I knew these things, when I felt them, I wept freely: for Kayla, for her family, and then for myself, for all the sorrows I can neither understand nor express.

For a time I was comforted by this precious gift of tears.

A few years after my epiphany at Kayla Ruth's memorial, my family and I were blessed by our adoption of an abused Chinese pug. Rue (a misspelling since her name sprang from the rolling howl she would utter when excited: roo…roo…roo) came to us emaciated and cowering after time spent being beaten by a former owner.

We nursed her to health and greatly invested ourselves in her. She became sleek and affectionate, the happiest animal I've ever seen.

Yet the past beatings had taken a terrible toll. Rue was prone to seizures, brain damage that left her drooling and dumb. We tried everything to heal her. But the seizures only worsened.

One night as I lay beside her on the carpet, I began to sob. Rue had been quivering and whimpering all evening, despite her medication. I felt so helpless. After such a great investment of time and effort, I had come to love Rue profoundly. My inability to comfort her was too much to bear. So I wept.

And my tears were an expression of the inexpressible. A futility I could never name. An ache too deep for words. No translation was required. Perfect prayer. And I was comforted.

On reflection, I realize that I had ceased to believe when yet a small boy because I felt I could not trust the God that allowed my dog to die. For twenty long years I had no need to cry because I had no need to pray to a non-existent God. Yet the pains of life eventually forced tears from me. And those tears began to heal me, ever so slowly. Spirit responded to each tear until the day of Rue's death. I came to believe once more through the precious gift of tears.

****

Friends, may you be blessed with tears:
Bitter tears to free you from your bondage;
Sorrowful tears to heal your wounds;
Tears of joy and love.
For all these things, and more, God gave us tears.

Afterthoughts

I was once told that in the end everything is okay, and that if it's not okay, it's not the end.
To see that tears are "okay," as are the pains and difficulties that precipitate them, is a tremendous learning for me.

Questions to Consider

Do I cry? For what reasons or causes? Am I comfortable with my tears? Do I see their value? If not, can I conceive of a value that is not obvious to me?

_____
_____
_____
_____
_____
_____
_____
_____

BELOVED

HER name is Jane, but I do not know what I should call her. Partner? Mate? Companion? Certainly not a girlfriend, and never the abominal phrase "significant other."

She was a client of my consulting services before Regina and I divorced. Jane was a friend for more than three years before we dated, the first occasion in my life of getting to know a woman well before crossing into intimacy. At the time we became involved many accusations were leveled from many directions, accusations of infidelity, which was quite ironic since both she and I had never approached a relationship more cleanly or honestly.

I came to appreciate and admire her from the safe vantage of friendship. I came to love Jane before I ever crossed the boundaries of friendship. Even thereafter, it unfolded as courtship, slowly and patiently.

Jane wrote an endearing piece to describe her experience. She included it with my Christmas gift.

****

Once upon a time there was a girl who had decided to live alone.

There was also a boy who loved the girl. The girl knew the boy was wonderful, but she was afraid.

The boy was very patient and just loved the girl though she had decided to be alone and was afraid. Occasionally the boy would ask the girl if she could love him the way he loved her.

She would reply, "I do love you, but you must only be my most special friend."

The boy would agree. He would quietly continue to love the girl and be her most special friend.

One day the girl said to the boy, "Someday, some girl will be very lucky to have you love them, because you are the most wonderful boy I have ever known."

And then the girl heard a voice. The voice said, "Yes, but why not you?"

The girl's heart softened. God was able to heal the fear, and the girl looked at the boy differently.

One day the boy asked the question again. "Do you think you could love me like I love you?"

The girl said, "Maybe I do."

The boy asked, "May I hold your hand?"

The girl replied, "Yes, I think that would be okay."

Sometime later, the boy asked another question. "Would it be okay if I kissed you?"

The girl said, "Yes, I believe that would be nice."

They kissed, and from that day forward, the Hand of God has held the boy and girl together, especially when they kiss.

****

Hers is such a lovely tale. I wish I could match it with some equally quaint story. But that does not seem to be my artistic flair. Instead I am an essayist, a commentator, an observer of that which surrounds me as a foundation for peering within myself.

Yet relating to Jane has shown me clearly my inner desires. All I ever wanted was to be cherished, to be free of criticism and loved simply as I am. I want to be seen, not as an illusion, but wholly as I am…beautiful, imperfect, emotionally and psychologically challenged, willing and trusting, supportive, childlike, selfish and yet oddly selfless. I want to cease the weary dance of romance and impression, and bask in the glory of love. I want to be loved.

Afterthoughts

I recall the ending of a lovely relationship. I couldn't say why it ended, it just couldn't go any further. I was done.

I lamented its passing. I asked Patrick why it had to be so hard, why there wasn't a shortcut.

I'll never forget his answer. "You can't know until you know. And you can't know without walking the path long enough in order to know."

Questions to Consider

There are only three choices available to us: being willing to do the work of my life with the persons currently in my life, being willing to do the work of my life but only with a change in those people in my life, and being unwilling to do the work of my life with anyone. Which of these best represents my state of mind today?

_____

_____

_____

_____

_____

_____

_____

Beyond his professional endeavors, Ron Chapman is a radio commentator and host of _Straight to the Heart: Radio Conversations_. He currently lives in New Mexico and loves its vistas, cuisine and cultures. Ron's passion is to see people's lives transformed.

In addition to _What a Wonderful World: Seeing Through New Eyes_, Ron has produced a compact disc entitled _Yes - It is a Wonderful World_! with four thought-provoking pieces. Winner of the 2001 National Federation of Press Women Award for Personal Radio Commentary as well as numerous speaking awards, Ron has received Toastmasters International's highest award of Distinguished Toastmaster. He holds a Masters Degree in Social Welfare from the University at Albany (New York) and a Bachelors Degree in Business from Valparaiso University.

His clientele includes governmental units such as the Centers for Disease Control and Prevention, private sector organizations including HealthSouth Corporation, the World Health Organization, the American Cancer Society - New England Division, and a number of local non-profit organizations and small businesses. You may contact Ron at www.magneticnorthllc.com with inquiries about speeches, workshops and personal and organizational development consulting.

A BIBLIOGRAPHY OF USEFUL THOUGHTS

AA World Services. *Alcoholics Anonymous*. New York: AA World Services, 1976.

Bach, Richard. *Illusions of a Reluctant Messiah*. New York: Dell Publishing, 1977.

Bach, Richard. *Jonathan Livingston Seagull*. New York: Avon, 1970.

Berry, Wendell. *The Hidden Wound*. San Francisco: North Point Press, 1989.

Borich, Judy. *Touch and Go the Nature of Intimacy: Relating in the Coming Times*. Interact Publishing, 2002.

Cohen, Alan. *The Dragon Doesn't Live Here Any More: Loving Fully, Living Freely*. Fawcett Books, 1993.

Davison, Todd. *Trust the Force: Change Your Life Through Attitudinal Healing*. Northvale, NJ: Jason Aronson Inc., 1995.

De Mello, Anthony. *Awareness*. Image Books, 1990.

DesMaisons, Kathleen. *Potatoes Not Prozac*. New York, Simon & Schuster, 1998.

Foundation for Inner Peace. *A Course in Miracles*. Glen Ellen, CA: Foundation for Inner Peace, 1975.

Gandhi, Mohandas K. *Gandhi: The Story of My Experiments with Truth*. New York, Beacon Press, 1957.

Gibson, Bob. *The Science of Mind* (Tape Series). Rhondell Publishing Company.

Glasser, William. *Control Theory*. New York: Harper & Row, 1984.

Goldsmith, Joel. *The Gift of Love*. San Francisco: Harper Collins, 1993.

Goldsmith, Joel. *The Thunder of Silence*. San Francisco: Harper Collins, 1993.

Harrison, Steven. *Doing Nothing: Coming to the End of the Spiritual Search*. New York: Putnam, 1997.

Kline, David. *Great Possessions: An Amish Farmer's Journal*. San Francisco, North Point Press, 1990.

Kundera, Milan. *The Unbearable Lightness of Being: A Novel*. Perrenial Press, 1999.

Levine, Stephen. *Turning Toward the Mystery*. San Francisco: Harper, 2002.

Levine, Stephen. *Who Dies?* New York: Doubleday, 1982.

May, Gerald G. *Addiction & Grace: Love and Spirituality in the Healing of Addictions*. San Francisco: Harper, 1988.

Millman, Dan. *The Way of the Peaceful Warrior*. Tiburon, CA: HJ Kramer Inc., 1980.

Nelson, Richard. *The Island Within*. San Francisco: North Point Press, 1989.

Quenk, Alex T. and Naomi L. *True Loves: Finding the Soul in Love Relationships*. Palo Alto: Davies Black Publishing, 1997.

Quinn, Daniel. *The Story of B*. New York: Bantam Books, 1996.

Roosevelt, Theodore. *Theodore Roosevelt: An Autobiography*. New York, De Capo Press, 1913.

Savory, Allan with Jody Butterfield. *Holistic Management: A New Framework for Decision Making*. Washington DC, Island Press, 1999.

Schaef, Anne Wilson. *Escape from Intimacy*. San Francisco, Harper Collins, 1989.

Steiner, Rudolph. *Knowledge of the Higher Worlds and its Attainment*. Spring Valley, NY: Anthroposophic Press, 1947.

Tolle, Eckhart. *The Power of Now: A Guide to Spiritual Enlightenment*. Novato, CA: New World Library, 1999.

Tolstoy, Leo. *The Kingdom of God is Within You*. Lincoln, NE: University of Nebraska Press, 1984.

Whitman, Walt. "Song of Myself" *Leaves of Grass*. New York: WW Norton & Company, 1965.

Williams, Terry Tempest. *Leap*. New York, Pantheon Books, 2000.

Williams, Terry Tempest. *Red: Passion and Patience in the Desert*. New York, Pantheon Books, 2001.

Williams, Terry Tempest. *Refuge: An Unnatural History of Family and Place*. Vintage Books, 1992.

Woolger, Roger. *Other Lives, Other Selves*. New York, Bantam Books, 1988.

Yogananda, Paramahansa. *Autobiography of a Yogi*. Los Angeles: Self Realization Fellowship, 1969.

ORDER FORM

You may purchase additional copies of *What a Wonderful World: Seeing Through New Eyes* as well as the compact disc, *Yes – It is a Wonderful World!*, at www.magneticnorthllc.com.

Or you may complete and use this order form, enclose your check or money order payable to Ron Chapman, and return to:

> **Magnetic North LLC**
> **2431 Northwest Circle NW**
> **Albuquerque, NM 87104**

Please allow two weeks for delivery via the United States Postal Service.

Name: _____

Shipping Address: _____

Shipping Address: _____

City: _____ **State:** _____ **Zip Code:** _____

By using this form from the book as proof of purchase, you'll receive the compact disc at a discount of $2.40 off the regular list price of $10.95.

Cost per book: Number _____ X $13.95 _____

Shipping and Handling _____ X $ 4.00 _____

Cost per compact disc Number _____ X $ 8.55 _____

Shipping and Handling _____ X $ 2.00 _____

Total Order _____

Printed in the United States
19645LVS00002B/115-254